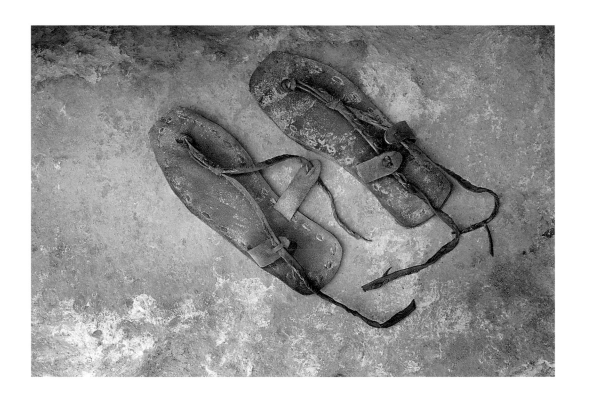

Where Jesus Walked

Then Jesus spoke to them again, saying,
"I am the light of the world. He who follows Me shall not walk in darkness,
but have the light of life."

JOHN 8:12

Success is not measured by what you've done. It's measured by who you've become.

ROBERT ANTHONY SCHULLER

INTEGRITY®
PUBLISHERS
Nashville

www.integritypublishers.com

PANOGRAPHS® BY KEN DUNCAN

OLIVE GROVE, BANIAS, CAESAREA PHILIPPI, ISRAEL

Jesus came to this area with his disciples. Here Peter gained a revelation of the true nature of Jesus as the Son of God.

It doesn't matter who or what is against you, because God is with you and always on your side!

ROBERT ANTHONY SCHULLER

DESIGN: PETER MORLEY, GOOD CATCH DESIGN
MAP ILLUSTRATIONS: JOHN BULL, THE BOOK DESIGN CO.
EDITING: PETER FRIEND
PHOTOGRAPHY: KEN DUNCAN
COPYRIGHT © 2006 DIVINE GUIDANCE PTY. LIMITED
REPROGRAPHICS: CFL PRINT STUDIO, AUSTRALIA.
www.createdforlife.com
PRODUCTION: PANOGRAPHS® PUBLISHING PTY. LIMITED,
A DIVISION OF THE KEN DUNCAN GROUP
PRINTED AND BOUND IN CHINA
ISBN 1-59145-588-X

FOR MORE INFORMATION ABOUT KEN DUNCAN AND HIS WORK
VISIT **www.kenduncan.com**

Front Cover
SUNRISE OVER THE SEA OF GALILEE, MOUNT
OF BEATITUDES, ISRAEL

Title Page
REPLICA SANDALS, SIMILAR TO THOSE JESUS
MIGHT HAVE WORN

Endpapers
MOSAIC, INTERIOR OF THE BASILICA OF THE
TRANSFIGURATION, MT. TABOR, ISRAEL

SUNRISE OVER THE SEA OF GALILEE FROM MOUNT ARBEL, ISRAEL

An ancient shepherd's path leads up to this high place from the Capernaum area. The Bible often refers to Jesus retreating to lonely places to pray and this could well have been a favorite location. The area has changed little since the time of Jesus.

Foreword

Be anxious for nothing,
but in everything by prayer and supplication, with thanksgiving,
let your requests be made known to God;
and the peace of God, which surpasses all understanding,
will guard your hearts and minds through Christ Jesus.

PHILIPPIANS 4:6–7

I have had the privilege of visiting the Holy Land dozens of times. Every time I travel to the region I am struck by the awesome fact that this is the land where Jesus Christ lived. The history of the Gospels comes alive for me. For Jesus is no myth; he is not just a figment of our religious imagination. His life, death and resurrection are firmly rooted in the history of a particular land. Many sites can still be visited and correlate closely with the documents of the New Testament. In fact, there exists today more conclusive evidence supporting the remarkable and life-changing events of Jesus' life than there is for many other ancient figures, including Caesar Augustus.

The value of this beautiful book by Ken Duncan is that it enables us, as the title states, to walk where Jesus walked. It offers us a chance to approach the Gospels *geographically*. Because of my own experiences in the Holy Land, I now find I cannot think of a passage in the Gospels without thinking at the same time of a particular geographic location. Walking in these places—or seeing the photographs in this book—expands our view by taking us 'on location', even at a distance of two thousand years. We see the mountains and valleys, the hillsides and villages, the roads and towns. We are able to get a sense of the distances between places, and of the character of diverse landscapes from Mount Hermon in the far north to the Dead Sea. The reality of the historical Jesus thus becomes far more vivid than we could otherwise imagine.

But we also see something else in the Holy Land. The land today is not merely the site of ancient Jewish remains. It is as multi-layered as history itself. It boasts everything from the earliest known man-made structure on the planet (the remnants of a 9000 year old tower in Jericho) to the highly sophisticated industries and cities of the modern Israelis. In the midst lie layer upon layer of Ancient Near East, Greek, Roman, Byzantine, Crusader and Islamic culture. It also retains, in modern times, an incredible religious diversity: Jewish, Christian and Muslim, each with their own long traditions and sacred sites.

This means that any pilgrimage to the Holy Land today will be very multi-dimensional. Sites from Jesus' time will be seen alongside—or under or within—a multiplicity of other historical and modern structures. The Temple Mount today is crowned with the Muslim Dome of the Rock. The manger site where Jesus was born in Bethlehem lies within a Byzantine basilica, which itself replaced a church built by Constantine's mother Helena. And so it goes on: layer upon layer, world within world. Sometimes it is difficult to sort out true history from centuries-old tradition. And yet still, as Ken Duncan's photos so vividly portray, we are left with a body of evidence about Jesus' life and times that is overwhelming.

As we know from the media, the region of the Holy Land is also a powder keg of great hostility and conflict, which recent events there have only confirmed. My hope and prayer is that this book will help spur many Christians to pray anew for peace in the Middle East. We read in the Gospels that Jesus stood and wept over Jerusalem. I have experienced this same kind of feeling. I have looked over the city of Jerusalem, knowing a little of its turbulent history and chaotic present, and I have wept. May you too be greatly and powerfully moved as you experience the Holy Land through the pages of this book, following in the footsteps of Jesus.

ROBERT ANTHONY SCHULLER. SENIOR PASTOR
CRYSTAL CATHEDRAL. HOUR OF POWER

Peace begins with you and me.
ROBERT ANTHONY SCHULLER

SUNSET AT NIMROD FORTRESS, VIEWED FROM MOUNT HERMON, ISRAEL

Nimrod Fortress is the largest and best preserved castle from the Crusader period. Banias is prominently located in the valley below.

Look for the light behind every shadow. ROBERT H. SCHULLER

DEDICATION

This book is dedicated to my best friend, Jesus. When I decided to walk with Him, the adventure of my life began.

KEN DUNCAN

FISHERMEN. SEA OF GALILEE. ISRAEL
Little has changed over the years for fishermen on the Sea of Galilee. They are still subject to the whims of nature, and the hours are long.

And as He walked by the Sea of Galilee, He saw Simon and Andrew his brother casting a net into the sea; for they were fishermen. Then Jesus said to them, "Follow Me, and I will make you become fishers of men." They immediately left their nets and followed Him.

MARK 1:16–18

BOUGAINVILLEA ON THE MOUNT OF BEATITUDES, SEA OF GALILEE, ISRAEL

Contents

God loves you and so do I: A powerful prescription for peace.
ROBERT H. SCHULLER

AQUEDUCT FROM ROMAN TIMES, CAESAREA, ISRAEL

Introduction

...Jesus stood and cried out, saying,
"If anyone thirsts, let him come to Me and drink.
He who believes in Me,
as the Scripture has said,
out of his heart will flow rivers of living water."

JOHN 7:37–38

Two important relationships have come together in the production of this unique book. The first is the wonderful friendship I enjoy with the Schuller family. Like many people, I first came to know Dr. Robert Schuller from afar, through the *Hour of Power* broadcasts in my home country of Australia. It was from Dr. Schuller that I learned to 'think positively' as a believer in Jesus Christ. This was a foundational message for me at the start of my Christian life, and one for which I continue to be deeply grateful.

Later I came to know Dr. Robert and Arvella Schuller personally, and experienced first hand their love, joy and faith. On several occasions I have been privileged to speak at the Crystal Cathedral. My friendship with Dr. Schuller's son, Reverend Robert Anthony Schuller, is now also very dear to me, and it is with great pleasure that we have collaborated to bring you this book following the 'footsteps' of Jesus.

The second important relationship in the birth of this book is my relationship with Integrity Publishers. This began after Mel Gibson invited me to take photographs on the set of the movie *The Passion of the Christ* in 2003. That project was one of the most exciting and emotionally challenging I have ever been involved in. The success of the resultant book in 2004 led to an invitation from Integrity to shoot a new project entitled 'Where Jesus Walked'. It was an invitation I immediately jumped at. I have long believed that the best way to get to know someone is to 'walk with them' awhile. Such a project would enable me to 'walk awhile' with the Christ of the Gospels, to discover the locations on earth where he lived and breathed, and to follow his progress from Bethlehem to the cross and beyond.

And so began one of the great adventures of my life. I traveled

through Israel and the Palestinian Territories, and into Jordan, Lebanon and Egypt. (The map on page 200 will give you some idea of the modern layout of the region.) On one occasion I was stopped by Hezbollah gunmen in southern Lebanon, and had a tricky time convincing them I was not an Israeli spy! But we eventually parted on amicable terms.

Using local guides I traveled to scores of ancient and historic sites and waded through a veritable mountain of research material to determine the most likely places Jesus visited. I found many locations were widely accepted by both scholars and laypeople and seemed to me to be unquestionable. Other sites were less certain, based only upon long tradition. The actual sequence of Jesus' various travels was determined by harmonizing, as best as possible, the Gospel accounts in Matthew, Mark, Luke and John. The main exceptions were the possible sites of the Holy Family's visit to Egypt— on which the Gospels themselves are silent—which could only be based on long-held traditions of the Coptic Orthodox Church. But much of the rest could be traced directly from the pages of Scripture, which came alive to me like never before.

The result was a journey like no other I have experienced. Walking by the Sea of Galilee, poking through the alleyways of Jerusalem, traveling the road to Jericho, climbing lofty Mount Hermon—it all combined to confront me with the great weight of evidence concerning the walk of Jesus towards the cross. I wondered how anyone could doubt Jesus' existence or purpose? What amazing love: that God should send His Son to live and die on the earth, and to rise again that we might have eternal life! I trust that the pictures of my journey, along with the accompanying Scriptures and text, will draw you also into a closer—and deeper—walk with Jesus.

Ken Duncan.

ACKNOWLEDGEMENTS

First I would like to thank my beautiful wife Pamela and wonderful daughter Jessica for their love and support. Many thanks to Charlie Asmar, my good friend and the greatest guide in Israel, Palestine and Jordan (charlieasmar@yahoo.com). Thank you to Safwat Elbanna for his fantastic assistance in Egypt.

Thank you to Janet and the wonderful team at CFL Print Studio for their assistance with the prepress work. Thank you to the whole enthusiastic team at Integrity Publishers. Also to Jim Riemann and the many others who helped along the way —God bless you all.

Patience, kindness, goodness, faithfulness, forgiveness, gentleness, self-control, love, joy and peace: these qualities are the fruit of people that know God.
KEN DUNCAN

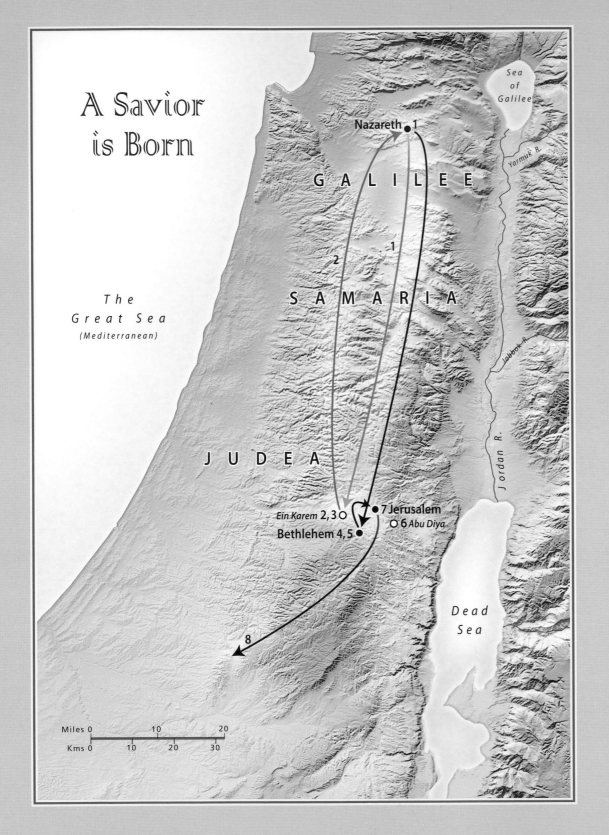

A Savior is Born

GALILEE

Nazareth 1

SAMARIA

The
Great Sea
(Mediterranean)

JUDEA

Ein Karem 2,3 ○
7 Jerusalem
○ 6 Abu Diya
Bethlehem 4,5 ●

Sea
of
Galilee

Yarmuk R.

Jabbok R.

Jordan R.

Dead
Sea

8

Miles 0 — 10 — 20
Kms 0 — 10 — 20 — 30

KEY

1. An angel appears to Mary in Nazareth, telling her that she will give birth to Jesus. Luke 1:26–38

2. Mary meets Elizabeth (the expectant mother of John the Baptist) in a country town of Judea traditionally identified as Ein Karem. Luke 1:39–56

3. John the Baptist is born (in Ein Karem, according to tradition) as the one called by God to make the way for Jesus. Luke 1:57–79

4. Jesus is born in Bethlehem. Matthew 2:1, Luke 2:1–7

5. Angels in a field near Bethlehem tell the shepherds of Jesus' birth. Luke 2:8–20

6. According to tradition, the wise men who came to see Jesus (Matthew 2:1–12) stayed in a cave on their return home, preserved now within St. Theodosius Monastery. The Monastery is located 12km east of Bethlehem at a town called Abu Diya.

7. Jesus is presented to the Lord at the temple in Jerusalem. Luke 2:22–39

8. The Holy Family escape to Egypt. Matthew 2:13–18

Lines show only general direction and approximate sequence of journeys.

⟶ Journey of Mary before Jesus' birth

⟶ Journey of Mary and Joseph

● Generally accepted or known location

○ Traditional location

MOSAIC, INTERIOR OF THE BASILICA OF THE TRANSFIGURATION,
MOUNT TABOR, ISRAEL

For whatever is born of God overcomes the world...

1 JOHN 5:4

A Savior is Born

I am a child of God and that's a somebody.   ROBERT H. SCHULLER

Brief descriptions and verbal sketches make up the Bible's account of Jesus' arrival. Tradition has supplied a host of further suggestions surrounding the Christmas story—but the heart remains the same: the birth of a baby like no other. All babies inspire great expectations. They arrive every day in our world. So what was so special about *this* baby, born in a wayside of the ancient Roman Empire? He arrived in the ordinary way, in circumstances that could hardly have been more humble. He was the "most expected" and yet the nature of his birth was the "least expected". Yet why shouldn't the Savior of the common man have chosen the commonest of births?

Jesus was a fulfillment of ancient promises. Words of God's faithfulness—spoken through the prophets of ancient Israel—echoed down through the centuries until that moment when "the Word became flesh and dwelt among us" (John 1:14). The familiar carol expresses it well: "Hark the herald angels sing: Glory to the new born King!"

THE MONASTERY OF SAINT GEORGE. WADI QELT. PALESTINE

The Monastery of Saint George, "Dair Al Qelt", clings to the canyon (wadi) walls like a fairy-tale castle. Wadi Qelt is a natural rift with high, sheer rock walls stretching between Jerusalem and Jericho. The narrow road lining the wadi was once the main way to Jericho. Tradition holds that Elijah stayed in a cave here, and that Joachim (Mary's father) came to this cave to pray for his infertile wife Anne. According to this tradition, an angel announced to him that they would have a child (Mary the mother of Jesus).

Where there's life, there's hope! ROBERT H. SCHULLER

15

MARY'S WELL. THE CHURCH OF SAINT GABRIEL.
NAZARETH. ISRAEL

*Then the angel said to her, "Do not be afraid,
Mary, for you have found favor with God. And
behold, you will conceive in your womb and bring
forth a Son, and shall call His name JESUS."*

LUKE 1:30–31

THE CHURCH OF SAINT GABRIEL, NAZARETH, ISRAEL
According to tradition, the angel Gabriel first appeared to Mary while she was drawing water from the well now protected inside this church.

Let your worry drain out and let God's peace flow in.

THE CHURCH OF THE VISITATION,
EIN KAREM, ISRAEL

This Church is said to stand on the site of the home of Elizabeth and Zacharias. When Mary came to visit them, Elizabeth's unborn baby—John the Baptist—was so affected that he leapt within Elizabeth's womb. Even before his birth, John knew the importance of this encounter. And in the future, it would be John's mission to prepare the way for Jesus. Their destinies were linked.

Now Mary arose in those days and went into the hill country with haste, to a city of Judah, and entered the house of Zacharias and greeted Elizabeth. And it happened, when Elizabeth heard the greeting of Mary, that the babe leaped in her womb; and Elizabeth was filled with the Holy Spirit. Then she spoke out with a loud voice and said, "Blessed are you among women, and blessed is the fruit of your womb!"

LUKE 1:39–42

The Lord is my light and my salvation;
Whom shall I fear?
The Lord is the strength of my life;
Of whom shall I be afraid?

PSALM 27:1

MARY MEETS ELIZABETH. THE CHURCH OF THE VISITATION. EIN KAREM. ISRAEL
This painting depicts the well in Ein Karem where, it is believed, Mary and Elizabeth met.

THE GROTTO, THE CHURCH OF JOHN THE BAPTIST,
EIN KAREM, ISRAEL
This grotto underneath the Church of John the Baptist is said to mark
the place where John was born.

There was a man sent from God, whose name was John.
This man came for a witness, to bear witness of the Light, that
all through him might believe. He was not that Light, but was
sent to bear witness of that Light.

JOHN 1:6–8

...John the Baptist came preaching in the wilderness of Judea, and saying, "Repent, for the kingdom of heaven is at hand!" For this is he who was spoken of by the prophet Isaiah, saying: "The voice of one crying in the wilderness: 'Prepare the way of the LORD; Make His paths straight.' "

MATTHEW 3:1–3

THE CHURCH OF JOHN THE BAPTIST, EIN KAREM, ISRAEL

SUNRISE AT BETHLEHEM, PALESTINE   The hills in the center background are believed to be where an angel appeared to the shepherds, telling them of Jesus' birth.

There are infinite possibilities in little beginnings when God is in them. ROBERT H. SCHULLER

THE CHURCH OF THE NATIVITY, BETHLEHEM, PALESTINE

The Church of the Nativity, built by Constantine the Great (AD 330), stands in the center of Bethlehem over a cave called the Holy Crypt, which according to Christian tradition is the place where Jesus was born. This is perhaps the oldest existing Christian church in the world.

THE GROTTO OF THE NATIVITY. THE CHURCH OF
THE NATIVITY. BETHLEHEM, PALESTINE
The silver fourteen-pointed star designates the spot where, it is
believed, Jesus was born. Jesus' birth was prophesied by Isaiah
hundreds of years earlier.

*Now the birth of Jesus Christ was as follows: After His mother
Mary was betrothed to Joseph, before they came together, she was
found with child of the Holy Spirit. Then Joseph her husband,
being a just man, and not wanting to make her a public example,
was minded to put her away secretly. But while he thought about
these things, behold, an angel of the Lord appeared to him in a
dream, saying, "Joseph, son of David, do not be afraid to take
to you Mary your wife, for that which is conceived in her is of
the Holy Spirit. And she will bring forth a Son, and you shall
call His name JESUS, for He will save His people from their
sins." So all this was done that it might be fulfilled which was
spoken by the Lord through the prophet, saying: "Behold, the
virgin shall be with child, and bear a Son, and they shall call
His name Immanuel," which is translated, "God with us."
Then Joseph, being aroused from sleep, did as the angel of the
Lord commanded him and took to him his wife, and did not
know her till she had brought forth her firstborn Son. And he
called His name JESUS.*

MATTHEW 1:18–25

Dreams survive in hope. ROBERT H. SCHULLER **25**

Joseph also went up from Galilee... to the city of David, which is called Bethlehem... to be registered with Mary, his betrothed wife, who was with child... while they were there, the days were completed for her to be delivered. And she brought forth her firstborn Son, and wrapped Him in swaddling cloths, and laid Him in a manger, because there was no room for them in the inn.

LUKE 2:4–7

And the Word became flesh and dwelt among us, and we beheld His glory, the glory as of the only begotten of the Father, full of grace and truth.

JOHN 1:14

For unto us a Child is born, unto us a Son is given; and the government will be upon His shoulder. And His name will be called Wonderful, Counselor, Mighty God, Everlasting Father, Prince of Peace.

ISAIAH 9:6

THE GROTTO OF THE NATIVITY, THE CHURCH OF THE NATIVITY, BETHLEHEM, PALESTINE
This grotto is a cave that was once used as a stable for animals—yet this humble location has been traditionally honored as the birthplace of Jesus.

God's dreams are always so large that they require His help to make them come true. ROBERT H. SCHULLER

"I am the good shepherd; and I know My sheep, and am known by My own. As the Father knows Me, even so I know the Father; and I lay down My life for the sheep... they will hear My voice; and there will be one flock and one shepherd. Therefore My Father loves Me, because I lay down My life that I may take it again. No one takes it from Me, but I lay it down of Myself. I have power to lay it down, and I have power to take it again. This command I have received from My Father." (Words of Jesus)

JOHN 10:14–18

A SHEPHERD ON A HILLSIDE. NOT FAR FROM BETHLEHEM. PALESTINE

A FRESCO IN THE SHEPHERDS FIELD CHURCH,
NEAR BETHLEHEM, PALESTINE

Now there were... shepherds living out in the fields, keeping watch over their flock by night. And behold, an angel of the Lord stood before them, and the glory of the Lord shone around them, and they were greatly afraid. Then the angel said to them, "Do not be afraid, for behold, I bring you good tidings of great joy which will be to all people. For there is born to you this day in the city of David a Savior, who is Christ the Lord."

LUKE 2:8–11

A star is best seen at night. ROBERT H. SCHULLER **29**

SAINT THEODOSIOS MONASTERY, EAST OF BETHLEHEM, PALESTINE
After visiting the Holy Family in Bethlehem, it is believed the Wise Men stayed in caves now located under this church.

A PAINTING OF THE WISE MEN. SAINT THEODOSIOS
MONASTERY, PALESTINE

*Now after Jesus was born in Bethlehem of Judea... behold,
wise men from the East came to Jerusalem, saying, "Where is
He who has been born King of the Jews? For we have seen His
star in the East and have come to worship Him." ...When they
saw the star, they rejoiced with exceeding great joy. And when
they had come into the house, they saw the young Child with
Mary His mother, and fell down and worshiped Him. And
when they had opened their treasures, they presented gifts to
Him: gold, frankincense, and myrrh.*

MATTHEW 2:1–2, 10–11

SOUTHERN STEPS OF THE HULDAH GATES, JERUSALEM

These steps lead up to the Huldah Gates and the temple. You can see part of the gate (now mostly blocked with stonework) where the walls intersect at the top of the steps. It is most likely that the Holy family entered into the temple via these steps when presenting Jesus to the Lord.

And when eight days were completed for the circumcision of the Child, His name was called JESUS, the name given by the angel before He was conceived in the womb. Now when the days of her purification... were completed, they brought Him to Jerusalem to present Him to the Lord

LUKE 2:21–22

THE TEMPLE MOUNT, JERUSALEM

Today the Temple Mount is adorned with Muslim mosques, the most notable being The Dome of the Rock as seen in this image. At the time of Jesus, this was the site of the magnificent Jewish temple built by King Herod. How ironic that the very person who built a temple to glorify God was the one who sought to destroy God's Son, the infant Jesus.

Truly, one person can make a difference! ROBERT H. SCHULLER   **33**

THE ANCIENT BATH HOUSE IN ONE OF HEROD'S PALACES, HERODION, PALESTINE

It came to King Herod's attention that wise men, following a star, had come to Jerusalem looking for the one born "King of the Jews". Disturbed by this threat to his position, Herod requested them to find this king and report back to him. The wise men found Jesus but were warned in a dream not to return to Herod. God knew the king's heart—that Herod only wanted to destroy Jesus.

God matches the dream to the dreamer. ROBERT H. SCHULLER

THE CHAPEL OF THE INNOCENTS,
BETHLEHEM, PALESTINE
These are said to be some of the bones of children massacred
as a result of Herod's decree.

*Then Herod, when he saw that he was deceived by the
wise men, was exceedingly angry; and he sent forth
and put to death all the male children who were in
Bethlehem and in all its districts, from two years old
and under, according to the time which he had
determined from the wise men.*

MATTHEW 2:16

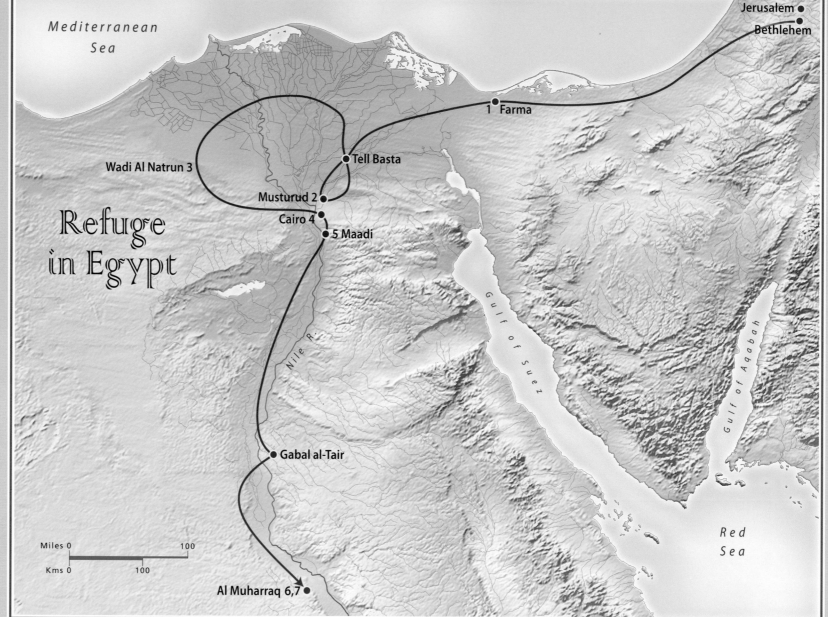

Mediterranean
Sea

Jerusalem
Bethlehem

**Refuge
in Egypt**

1 Farma

Wadi Al Natrun 3

Tell Basta

Musturud 2

Cairo 4

5 Maadi

Nile R.

Gulf of Suez

Gulf of Aqabah

Gabal al-Tair

Red
Sea

Al Muharraq 6,7

Miles 0   100

Kms 0   100

KEY

Note: Although the Bible
includes several references to
Jesus' and his family's journey
to Egypt, no specific details
about the length of their
visit or particular places are
recorded. The following information is a brief selection
of some events preserved
in ancient Coptic Christian
tradition.

According to Coptic tradition:

1. The Holy Family stayed in an inn at Farma (ancient Pelusium).

2. Jesus created a well at Musturud, which the Holy Family
used for drinking, washing and bathing.

3. Jesus created a well at Al Hamra Lake, Wadi Al Natrun.

4. The Holy Family stayed in Old Cairo.

5. The Holy Family crossed the Nile at Maadi.

6. The Holy Family's longest stay in Egypt was at Al Muharraq.

7. An angel appeared to Joseph while at Al Muharraq and
told him to return home to Israel. Matthew 2:19–20

Lines show only general direction and approximate
sequence of journeys.

⟶ Supposed route of the Holy Family
through Egypt, according to Coptic Orthodox tradition

● Important sites associated with the Holy Family,
according to Coptic Orthodox tradition

MOSAIC OF THE HOLY FAMILY, MUSTURUD, EGYPT

...behold, an angel of the Lord appeared to Joseph in a dream, saying,
"Arise, take the young Child and His mother, flee to Egypt, and stay there until I bring you word..."

MATTHEW 2:13

Refuge in Egypt

Be bold, courage isn't feeling free from fear; courage is facing fears you feel!   ROBERT H. SCHULLER

When threatened, it is only natural to seek an escape: The higher the stakes, the greater the need for refuge. When Herod determined to destroy the infant Christ, God answered by revealing to Joseph in a dream that he should take the child and his mother and "flee to Egypt". It was a sojourn shrouded in mystery. Where in Egypt did they go? What impact, if any, did they have on the Egyptian inhabitants? The Gospel account passes over such questions and leaps forward instead to the return of the Holy Family to Israel. It was there, in the land of the Jews, that the great drama of God's coming Kingdom was to be unfolded.

Yet if you visit Egypt today, you will hear many stories about Jesus' time in the Land of the Nile. They are strange tales to Western ears—stories of trees bending in homage to the Christ Child, and wells miraculously appearing in the Egyptian barrenness. Many such sites are now venerated by Coptic Orthodox believers, with traditions that may be traced to medieval times or even earlier. How did these traditions begin? Are any true? We don't really know. We only know for certain that Mary, Joseph and Jesus stayed in Egypt until Joseph's next momentous dream, telling them to return.

ANCIENT CHURCH RUINS, 5TH–7TH CENTURY, FARMA, EGYPT

These ancient church remains are built on the site of a village where it is believed the Holy Family stayed. The number of churches on this site gives credence to the importance of the location for early pilgrims. According to historical sources, Coptic Christianity can be traced as far back as St. Mark (the writer of the second Gospel) who became the first bishop of Alexandria in the middle of the first century.

OIL LAMP FROM THE TIME OF JESUS, FARMA, EGYPT
This lamp was excavated from the remains of the early village.
Perhaps this very lamp was used by the Holy Family!

*"I have come as a light into the world, that whoever believes
in Me should not abide in darkness." (Words of Jesus)*

JOHN 12:46

YOUNG WOMAN, AL HAMRA LAKE,
WADI AL NATRUN, EGYPT
Two thousand years on, a woman of similar age to Mary watches
over a child swimming. Perhaps Jesus too swam in this lake.

For this is the message that you heard from the beginning,
that we should love one another.

1 JOHN 3:11

MARY'S SPRING, AL HAMRA LAKE,
WADI AL NATRUN, EGYPT

Coptic Christian tradition holds that Jesus touched this salty
lake and fresh water came up as a spring. This spring was later
encased to protect the valuable fresh water. It has never dried up,
and to this day it is still used by the locals.

JOHN 4:14

"But whoever drinks of the water
that I shall give him will never thirst...
the water that I shall give him will become in him a
fountain of water springing up into everlasting life."
(Words of Jesus)

JOHN 4:14

SUNRISE AT THE PYRAMIDS OF GIZA, EGYPT   The Holy Family may have passed these ancient wonders of the world on their journey through Old Cairo.

Build a dream and the dream will build you. ROBERT H. SCHULLER

STAIRCASE TO THE CRYPT OF THE HOLY FAMILY, THE CHURCH
OF ABU SERGA, OLD CAIRO, EGYPT

It is said that when the Holy Family entered Old Cairo, the presence of Jesus, even as a
child, was so powerful it caused the pagan idols to fall down. According to this story, the
local governor was so enraged that the Holy Family had to seek shelter in the cave that
now lies beneath the Church of Abu Serga. The Coptic Christians see this and other similar
events as a fulfillment of the prophecy of Isaiah 19:1.

FELUCCA SAILING ON THE NILE RIVER. MAADI. EGYPT
After the Holy Family's short stay in Old Cairo (according to tradition) they boarded
a sailing boat at Maadi and headed up the Nile.

*Behold, the L*ORD* rides on a swift cloud,*
And will come into Egypt;
The idols of Egypt will totter at His presence,
And the heart of Egypt will melt in its midst.

ISAIAH 19:1

THE MONASTERY OF AL MUHARRAQ, EGYPT

According to tradition, the Holy Family's longest stay was at Al Muharraq, where they were well received. It was at this place, tradition says, that the angel appeared to Joseph (the father of Jesus) and told him it was safe to return to Israel.

THE ROOM OF THE HOLY FAMILY, THE
MONASTERY OF AL MUHARRAQ, EGYPT
According to Coptic tradition, the Holy Family stayed in this
room. Here there is a stone said to be the resting place of
Jesus as a child. Lying in the very midst of Egypt, this stone
is now an altar which the Copts believe is the fulfillment
of Isaiah 19:19–20.

*In that day there will be an altar to the LORD in the
midst of the land of Egypt, and a pillar to the LORD
at its border. And it will be for a sign and for a witness
to the LORD of hosts in the land of Egypt...*

ISAIAH 19:19–20

*Now when Herod was dead, behold, an angel of the Lord appeared in a dream to Joseph in Egypt, saying, "Arise,
take the young Child and His mother, and go to the land of Israel, for those who sought the young Child's life are
dead." Then he arose, took the young Child and His mother, and came into the land of Israel.* MATTHEW 2:19–21

Your dream is God's gift to you. ROBERT H. SCHULLER **47**

ROMAN AQUEDUCT, CAESAREA, ISRAEL

The Holy Family would have passed this aqueduct on their return to Nazareth if, as is thought, they took the coast road.

Stay focused on your dream. ROBERT H. SCHULLER

HEROD'S HIPPODROME, CAESAREA, ISRAEL

This hippodrome was part of the magnificent coastal city (Caesarea) built by Herod the Great. Perhaps the Holy Family stopped here on their way back from Egypt?

Lord be the pilot that guides and controls my life. ROBERT H. SCHULLER

SUNSET OVER NAZARETH, ISRAEL

Beloved, let us love one another, for love is of God; and everyone who loves is born of God and knows God. He who does not love does not know God, for God is love. In this the love of God was manifested toward us, that God has sent His only begotten Son into the world, that we might live through Him. In this is love, not that we loved God, but that He loved us and sent His Son to be the propitiation [the means of warding off the justifiable anger of God] for our sins. Beloved, if God so loved us, we also ought to love one another.

1 JOHN 4:7–11

THE HOLY GROTTO. CHURCH OF THE ANNUNCIATION.
NAZARETH. ISRAEL

This church is built over the Holy Grotto, where, it is said, the angel
Gabriel appeared to Mary. It is also believed this is where Mary, Joseph
and Jesus lived on their return to Nazareth.

...they returned to Galilee, to their own city, Nazareth.
And the Child grew and became strong in spirit, filled with
wisdom; and the grace of God was upon Him.

LUKE 2:39–40

OLD CARPENTRY WORKSHOP, NAZARETH, ISRAEL
Nazareth Village has been constructed as authentically as possible to give visitors an understanding of the life and times of Jesus.

And Jesus increased in wisdom and stature, and in favor with God and men.

LUKE 2:52

CARPENTRY TOOLS, NAZARETH VILLAGE, NAZARETH, ISRAEL

These carpenter's tools are replicas of ones used in the days of Jesus. It is presumed Jesus
would have used such tools in his father's business.

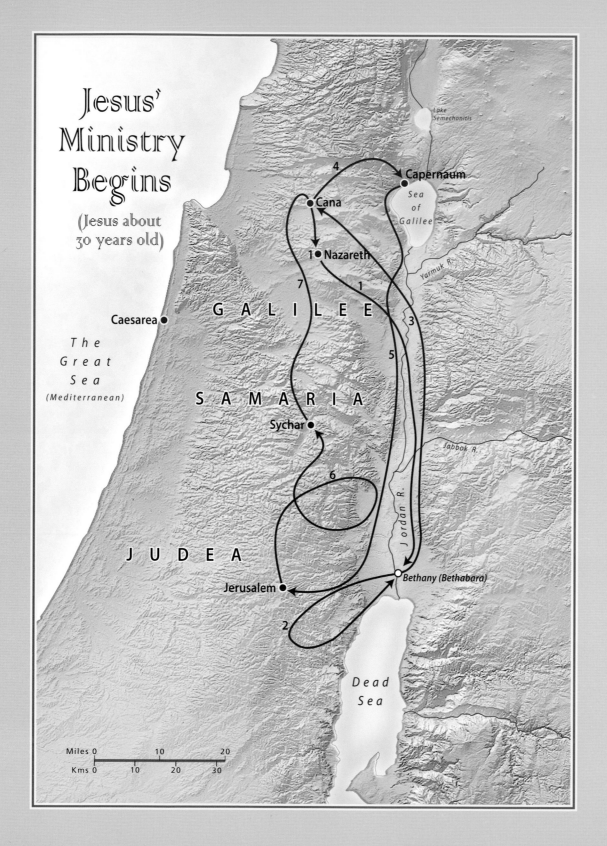

Jesus' Ministry Begins

(Jesus about 30 years old)

Lake Semechonitis

Capernaum

Cana

Sea of Galilee

Nazareth

Caesarea

The Great Sea (Mediterranean)

G A L I L E E

Yarmuk R.

S A M A R I A

Sychar

Jabbok R.

J U D E A

Jordan R.

Jerusalem

Bethany (Bethabara)

Dead Sea

Miles 0 10 20
Kms 0 10 20 30

KEY

1. Jesus leaves Nazareth and travels to the Jordan River to be baptized by John the Baptist. Matthew 3:13, Mark 1:9

2. Jesus is tempted in the wilderness (traditionally believed to be at the Mount of Temptations near Jericho). Matthew 4:1–11, Mark 1:12–13, Luke 4:1–13

3. From the wilderness, Jesus goes via Bethabara to Cana, where He turns the water into wine. John 2:1–11

4. Jesus travels from Cana to Capernaum. John 2:12

5. Jesus travels to Jerusalem for the Passover. John 2:13–25

6. Jesus travels through the Judean countryside (John 3:22) and then comes to Jacob's Well at Sychar in Samaria. Here, He meets the woman at the well. John 4:1–42

7. Jesus returns via Cana to Nazareth. Luke 4:16

Lines show only general direction and approximate sequence of journeys.

→ Jesus' Journey

● Generally accepted or known location

○ Possible location

PAINTING OF JESUS TURNING WATER INTO WINE,
FRANCISCAN CHURCH, KFAR KANA (CANA), ISRAEL

John [the Baptist] saw Jesus coming toward him, and said,
"Behold! The Lamb of God who takes away the sin of the world!"

JOHN 1:29

Jesus' Ministry Begins

If you can believe it you can achieve it.   ROBERT H. SCHULLER

People often take journeys to find themselves. Jesus journeyed to find us. Every step He took seemed purposeful: from His baptism in the Jordan and His temptation in the wilderness to His first miracle in Cana of Galilee. And yet there was also often a sense of mystery. Why, for instance, did Jesus choose a wedding in Cana for His first miraculous sign? And why did He turn the water there into wine? Was He trying to tell us something even at the very beginning of His ministry—that

wine, symbolic of blood, was somehow central to His unfolding purpose on the earth?

Jesus knew His own identity. He understood His reason for being here. His walk was a "working journey"—a search and rescue mission for those who were lost. We were the lost ones. He found people like us everywhere He went. Those who were paying attention heard Him express His purpose: in words, in symbols and in actions. He caught their attention, and said, "Follow me."

JESUS' BAPTISM SITE, KASR EL YEHUD, JORDAN RIVER, PALESTINE

Kasr El Yehud is believed to be where Jesus was baptized by John the Baptist. In Jesus' day the level of the river would have been higher. These days, much of the water upstream is diverted for irrigation.

It came to pass in those days that Jesus came from Nazareth of Galilee, and was baptized by John in the Jordan. And immediately, coming up from the water, He saw the heavens parting and the Spirit descending upon Him like a dove. Then a voice came from heaven, "You are My beloved Son, in whom I am well pleased."

MARK 1:9–11

Let your dreams, not your regrets, take command of your life. ROBERT H. SCHULLER

Then Jesus was led up by the Spirit into the wilderness to be tempted by the devil. And when He had fasted forty days and forty nights, afterward He was hungry. Now when the tempter came to Him, he said, "If You are the Son of God, command that these stones become bread." But He answered and said, "It is written, 'Man shall not live by bread alone, but by every word that proceeds from the mouth of God.'"

MATTHEW 4:1–4

THE JUDEAN WILDERNESS

Obstacles are opportunities in disguise. ROBERT H. SCHULLER

VIEW FROM THE MOUNT OF TEMPTATION, JERICHO, PALESTINE

The so-called Mount of Temptation is thought to be where Satan took Jesus to show Him the kingdoms of the world. If so, it is amusing to think that Satan has Jesus looking down over Jericho, the very city whose walls tumbled at God's command. Here Satan was offering Jesus something that could never be a match for God's almighty power.

TEMPLE PINNACLE, JERUSALEM
This site is thought to be the place of Jesus' second temptation.

*Then the devil took Him up into the holy city, set
Him on the pinnacle of the temple, and said to Him,
"If You are the Son of God, throw Yourself down.
For it is written: 'He shall give His angels charge
over you,' and, 'In their hands they shall bear you
up, lest you dash your foot against a stone.'"
Jesus said to him, "It is written again, 'You shall
not tempt the LORD your God.'"*

MATTHEW 4:5–7

When you're down—look up! It's impossible to feel down when you're looking up! ROBERT ANTHONY SCHULLER

MOUNT OF TEMPTATION, NEAR JERICHO, PALESTINE

Again, the devil took Him up on an exceedingly high mountain, and showed Him all the kingdoms of the world and their glory. And he said to Him, "All these things I will give You if You will fall down and worship me." Then Jesus said to him, "Away with you, Satan! For it is written, 'You shall worship the LORD your God, and Him only you shall serve.'" Then the devil left Him, and behold, angels came and ministered to Him.

MATTHEW 4:8–11

I will lift up my eyes to the hills— From whence comes my help? My help comes from the LORD, *who made heaven and earth.* PSALM 121:1–2

Courage is spelled I-N-T-E-G-R-I-T-Y. ROBERT H. SCHULLER **65**

THE MONASTERY OF THE TEMPTATION. MOUNT OF TEMPTATION. PALESTINE
The Stone of Temptation, on which Jesus is said to have sat, is enclosed inside the Monastery of the Temptation. This monastery has been built on the cliff side where it is believed Jesus was tempted by Satan.

Watch and pray, lest you enter into temptation. The spirit indeed is willing, but the flesh is weak.

MARK 14:38

Tough times never last, but . . . tough people do! ROBERT H. SCHULLER

67

STONE VESSEL, THE GREEK ORTHODOX CHURCH, CANA, ISRAEL

This church has two of the stone vessels believed to have been used in the wedding miracle at Cana where Jesus turned water into wine. There were six of these vessels. Looking at their size, it must have been a big celebration!

THE FRANCISCAN CHURCH, CANA, ISRAEL

This church in the center of Cana is believed to be built on the site of the house where the marriage was celebrated. There are stairs leading to excavations below the church. Here, visitors can see an old stone vessel, claimed to be another of the six used by Jesus when He turned water into wine.

On the third day there was a wedding in Cana of Galilee, and the mother of Jesus was there. Now both Jesus and His disciples were invited to the wedding. And when they ran out of wine, the mother of Jesus said to Him, "They have no wine."...His mother said to the servants, "Whatever He says to you, do it." Now there were set there six waterpots of stone, according to the manner of purification of the Jews, containing twenty or thirty gallons apiece. Jesus said to them, "Fill the waterpots with water." And they filled them up to the brim. And He said to them, "Draw some out now, and take it to the master of the feast." And they took it. When the master of the feast had tasted the water that was made wine, and did not know where it came from (but the servants who had drawn the water knew), the master of the feast called the bridegroom. And he said to him, "Every man at the beginning sets out the good wine, and when the guests have well drunk, then the inferior. You have kept the good wine until now!" This beginning of signs Jesus did in Cana of Galilee, and manifested His glory; and His disciples believed in Him.

JOHN 2:1–11

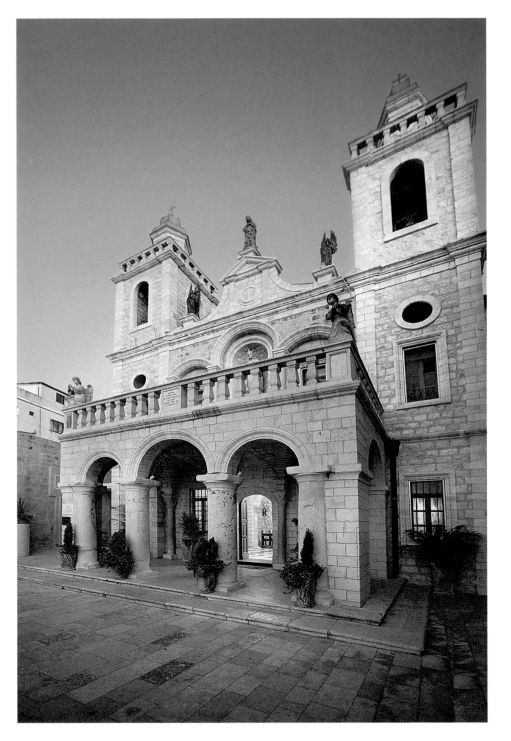

SYNAGOGUE, CAPERNAUM, ISRAEL

This is believed to be the synagogue in Capernaum where Jesus taught. Jesus lived in Capernaum for some time, using it as a base from which He traveled throughout Galilee.

Then He went down to Capernaum, a city of Galilee, and was teaching them on the Sabbaths. And they were astonished at His teaching, for His word was with authority. Now in the synagogue there was a man who had a spirit of an unclean demon. And he cried out with a loud voice, saying, "Let us alone! What have we to do with You, Jesus of Nazareth? Did You come to destroy us? I know who You are—the Holy One of God!" But Jesus rebuked him, saying, "Be quiet, and come out of him!" And when the demon had thrown him in their midst, it came out of him and did not hurt him. Then they were all amazed and spoke among themselves, saying, "What a word this is! For with authority and power He commands the unclean spirits, and they come out." And the report about Him went out into every place in the surrounding region.

LUKE 4:31–37

The Sabbath should be a time when hope is reborn, dreams are rekindled, self-worth restored.
ROBERT H. SCHULLER

FISHERMEN ON THE SEA OF GALILEE, ISRAEL

The character of fishermen on the Sea of Galilee has changed little since the time of Christ.
Two thousand years ago, men such as these were so impacted by Jesus that they left
everything to follow Him.

BIRDS RESTING, SEA OF GALILEE, ISRAEL

*And He [Jesus] was preaching in the synagogues of Galilee.
So it was, as the multitude pressed about Him to hear the
word of God, that He stood by the Lake of Gennesaret, and
saw two boats standing by the lake; but the fishermen had
gone from them and were washing their nets. Then He got
into one of the boats, which was Simon's, and asked him to
put out a little from the land. And He sat down and taught
the multitudes from the boat. When He had stopped speaking,
He said to Simon, "Launch out into the deep and let down
your nets for a catch." But Simon answered and said to
Him, "Master, we have toiled all night and caught nothing;
nevertheless at Your word I will let down the net." And when
they had done this, they caught a great number of fish, and
their net was breaking. So they signaled to their partners in
the other boat to come and help them. And they came and
filled both the boats, so that they began to sink. When Simon
Peter saw it, he fell down at Jesus' knees, saying, "Depart
from me, for I am a sinful man, O Lord!" For he and all
who were with him were astonished at the catch of fish which
they had taken; and so also were James and John, the sons
of Zebedee, who were partners with Simon. And Jesus said
to Simon, "Do not be afraid. From now on you will catch
men." So when they had brought their boats to land, they
forsook all and followed Him.*

LUKE 4:44–5:11

SUNRISE OVER JERUSALEM

Now when He was in Jerusalem at the Passover, during the feast, many believed in His name when they saw the signs which He did. JOHN 2:23

No person can succeed without helping people. ROBERT H. SCHULLER **75**

WATER JAR FROM THE TIME OF CHRIST

JACOB'S WELL, SYCHAR (NABLUS), SAMARIA, PALESTINE

This is the well where it is believed Jesus met with a Samaritan woman (see page 79 for the story). The well is now protected by a church, which has been built over it. To this day, the water from the well is crystal clear and beautiful to drink.

There is no thrill like the thrill of making a great discovery. God hides the greatest treasures in the places we least expect. ROBERT H. SCHULLER **77**

THE CHURCH OF JACOB'S WELL, SYCHAR (NABLUS), SAMARIA, PALESTINE

So He came to a city of Samaria which is called Sychar...
Now Jacob's well was there. Jesus... wearied from His journey,
sat thus by the well... A woman of Samaria came to draw
water. Jesus said to her, "Give me a drink."... the woman of
Samaria said to Him, "How is it that You, being a Jew, ask
a drink from me, a Samaritan woman?" For Jews have no
dealings with Samaritans. Jesus answered... "If you knew
the gift of God, and who it is who says to you, 'Give Me a
drink,' you would have asked Him, and He would have given
you living water." The woman said to Him, "Sir, You have
nothing to draw with, and the well is deep. Where then do
You get that living water? Are You greater than our father
Jacob, who gave us the well?... Jesus... said to her, "Whoever
drinks of this water will thirst again, but whoever drinks of
the water that I shall give him will never thirst. But the water
that I shall give him will become in him a fountain of water
springing up into everlasting life." The woman said to Him,
"Sir, give me this water, that I may not thirst..."

JOHN 4:5–15

There is no hopeless situation, until you become a hopeless person.   ROBERT H. SCHULLER

Trust in the LORD with all your heart,
And lean not on your own understanding;
In all your ways acknowledge Him,
And He shall direct your paths.
Do not be wise in your own eyes;
Fear the LORD and depart from evil.
It will be health to your flesh,
And strength to your bones.
Honor the LORD with your possessions,
And with the firstfruits of all your increase;
So your barns will be filled with plenty,
And your vats will overflow with new wine.

PROVERBS 3:5–10

REPLICA OF A WINE SKIN FROM THE TIME OF JESUS

REPLICA OF A WEAVER'S LOOM FROM THE TIME
OF JESUS

*The disciples of John and of the Pharisees were fasting. Then
they came and said to Him, "Why do the disciples of John
and of the Pharisees fast, but Your disciples do not fast?"
And Jesus said to them, "Can the friends of the bridegroom
fast while the bridegroom is with them? As long as they have
the bridegroom with them they cannot fast. But the days will
come when the bridegroom will be taken away from them,
and then they will fast in those days. No one sews a piece of
unshrunk cloth on an old garment; or else the new piece pulls
away from the old, and the tear is made worse. And no one
puts new wine into old wineskins; or else the new wine bursts
the wineskins, the wine is spilled, and the wineskins are
ruined. But new wine must be put into new wineskins."*

MARK 2:18–22

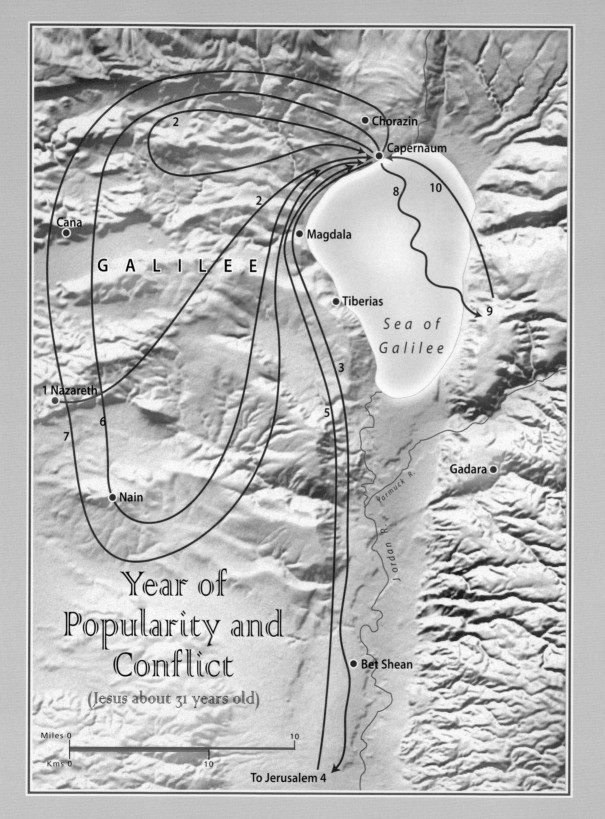

Year of Popularity and Conflict

(Jesus about 31 years old)

GALILEE

Chorazin

Capernaum

Cana

Magdala

Tiberias

Sea of Galilee

1 Nazareth

Nain

Gadara

Yarmuck R.

Jordan R.

Bet Shean

To Jerusalem 4

Miles 0 ————————— 10
Kms 0 ————————— 10

PAINTING, SAINT BISHOI MONASTERY,
WADI AL NATRUN

I am the good shepherd.
The good shepherd gives His life for the sheep. (Words of Jesus)

JOHN 10:11

THE JOURNEY CONTINUES

Year of Popularity and Conflict

Face your fears. Don't run from them. ROBERT H. SCHULLER

The short years of Jesus' ministry featured a continual ebb and flow of popularity and animosity. At first, His charismatic presence attracted curious and adoring crowds. The rising tide of popularity seemed unstoppable. Those who opposed Jesus didn't fear Him; they feared the crowds. But there was always an undertow of doubt, fear, jealousy, and disagreement over His identity and power. It is still the same. Today's adoring crowd may turn into tomorrow's lynch mob.

Early in Jesus' public ministry, the fickleness of fame displayed itself when He visited His home town of Nazareth. Luke 4:14–30 describes the encounter. In the synagogue, Jesus read a passage from the scroll of Isaiah and applied the message to Himself. He soon realized that people weren't listening very carefully. They found His words interesting, but not compelling. They merely wanted some miracles for their entertainment.

Jesus confronted their assumptions and shattered their feelings of privilege. Within moments the crowd's emotion had turned to a murderous rage. The one miracle Jesus worked in Nazareth that day was to walk away unharmed by the mob.

PAINTING, SYNAGOGUE CHURCH, NAZARETH, ISRAEL

This painting depicts Jesus reading scripture and preaching from a scroll. This church is built on the site of what is believed to be the original synagogue in Nazareth. (See page 87 for the Biblical account of this event.)

THE MOUNT OF THE PRECIPICE, NEAR NAZARETH, ISRAEL
Jesus enraged some of the inhabitants of Nazareth by His preaching.
They tried to throw Him off this precipice to kill Him, but He was supernaturally delivered. It was not the time for Jesus' life to be given.

God is stronger and bigger than my problem. ROBERT H. SCHULLER **85**

THE CHURCH OF THE SEVEN APOSTLES. CAPERNAUM. SEA OF GALILEE. ISRAEL

News of Jesus' miracles in Capernaum spread throughout Galilee and beyond. When Jesus visited Nazareth (his home town), the local inhabitants wanted to see the same miracles.
But their limited vision of Jesus hindered any major manifestation of His power. They still saw Him only as the carpenter's son.

So He came to Nazareth, where He had been brought up... He went into the synagogue on the Sabbath day, and stood up to read the book of the prophet Isaiah... He found the place where it was written: "The Spirit of the LORD is upon Me, because He has anointed Me to preach the gospel to the poor; He has sent Me to heal the brokenhearted, to proclaim liberty to the captives and recovery of sight to the blind, to set at liberty those who are oppressed; to proclaim the acceptable year of the LORD." Then He closed the book... and sat down. And the eyes of all who were in the synagogue were fixed on Him. And He began to say to them, "Today this Scripture is fulfilled in your hearing." So all bore witness to Him, and marveled at the gracious words which proceeded out of His mouth. And they said, "Is this not Joseph's son?" He said to them, "You will surely say this proverb to Me, 'Physician, heal yourself! Whatever we have heard done in Capernaum, do also here in Your country.' " Then He said, "Assuredly, I say to you, no prophet is accepted in his own country..." So all those in the synagogue, when they heard these things, were filled with wrath... and they led Him to the brow of the hill... that they might throw Him down over the cliff. Then passing through the midst of them, He went His way.

LUKE 4:16–30

You are God's project and God never fails.   ROBERT H. SCHULLER

THE THEATER IN BET SHEAN, ISRAEL

Bet Shean is an ancient city, located between Galilee and Jerusalem. It is a place Jesus would almost certainly have seen.

For I am persuaded that neither death nor life, nor angels nor principalities nor powers, nor things present nor things to come, nor height nor depth, nor any other created thing, shall be able to separate us from the love of God which is in Christ Jesus our Lord. ROMANS 8:38–39

THE POOL OF BETHESDA, JERUSALEM

...Jesus went up to Jerusalem. Now there is in Jerusalem by the Sheep Gate a pool, which is called in Hebrew, Bethesda, having five porches. In these lay a great multitude of sick people, blind, lame, paralyzed, waiting for the moving of the water. For an angel went down at a certain time into the pool and stirred up the water; then whoever stepped in first, after the stirring of the water, was made well of whatever disease he had. Now a certain man was there who had an infirmity thirty-eight years. When Jesus saw him lying there, and knew that he already had been in that condition a long time, He said to him, "Do you want to be made well?" The sick man answered Him, "Sir, I have no man to put me into the pool when the water is stirred up; but while I am coming, another steps down before me." Jesus said to him, "Rise, take up your bed and walk." And immediately the man was made well, took up his bed, and walked.

JOHN 5:1–9

WALKWAY IN FRONT OF THE SAINT ANNE CHURCH, NEAR THE POOL OF BETHESDA, JERUSALEM, ISRAEL
The Church of Saint Anne is built on the remains of a Byzantine church. It commemorates the traditional site of Mary's birthplace at the home of her parents Anne and Joachim.

...God anointed Jesus of Nazareth with the Holy Spirit and with power, who went about doing good and healing all who were oppressed... for God was with Him. ACTS 10:38

And seeing the multitudes, He went up on a mountain, and when
He was seated... He opened His mouth and taught them, saying:
Blessed are the poor in spirit,
For theirs is the kingdom of heaven.
Blessed are those who mourn,
For they shall be comforted.
Blessed are the meek,
For they shall inherit the earth.
Blessed are those who hunger and thirst for righteousness,
For they shall be filled.
Blessed are the merciful,
For they shall obtain mercy.
Blessed are the pure in heart,
For they shall see God.
Blessed are the peacemakers,
For they shall be called sons of God.
Blessed are those who are persecuted for righteousness' sake,
For theirs is the kingdom of heaven.

MATTHEW 5:1–10

SUNRISE OVER THE SEA OF GALILEE, MOUNT OF BEATITUDES, ISRAEL

This is the area where Jesus preached his famous Sermon on the Mount. Thousands came to hear Him. What a beautiful place to preach, in the midst of God's wonderful creation.

Faith is the natural blossom of someone who loves. ROBERT H. SCHULLER **93**

PAINTING OF THE MIRACLE OF THE WIDOW'S SON, NAIN CHURCH, ISRAEL

This painting, displayed in the Nain Church, helps transport us back to the time when Jesus raised a widow's son from the dead.

He [Jesus] went into a city called Nain... And when He came near the gate of the city, behold, a dead man was being carried out, the only son of his mother; and she was a widow... When the Lord saw her, He had compassion on her and said to her, "Do not weep." Then He came and touched the open coffin, and those who carried him stood still. And He said, "Young man, I say to you, arise." So he who was dead sat up and began to speak. And He presented him to his mother. Then fear came upon all, and they glorified God, saying, "A great prophet has risen up among us"; and, "God has visited His people."

LUKE 7:11–16

EXTERIOR OF NAIN CHURCH, ISRAEL
This church is built on the site where it is traditionally believed that Jesus healed the widow's son.

[Jesus said] "A new commandment I give to you, that you love one another; as I have loved you, that you also love one another. By this all will know that you are My disciples, if you have love for one another."

JOHN 13:34–35

Now it came to pass, afterward, that He [Jesus] went through every city and village, preaching and bringing the glad tidings of the kingdom of God. And the twelve were with Him, and certain women who had been healed of evil spirits and infirmities—Mary called Magdalene, out of whom had come seven demons, and Joanna the wife of Chuza, Herod's steward, and Susanna, and many others who provided for Him from their substance.

LUKE 8:1–3

VIEW FROM MT ARBEL, OVERLOOKING THE AREA OF MAGDALA AND SEA OF GALILEE, ISRAEL
Magdala was the birthplace of Mary Magdalene, whom Jesus met and delivered from seven evil spirits.
Mary was so appreciative of the transformation in her life that she became a great believer, follower and supporter of Jesus Christ.

Faith is always stronger than failure.   ROBERT H. SCHULLER

CALM SUNRISE, SEA OF GALILEE, TIBERIAS, ISRAEL

... He [Jesus] got into a boat with His disciples. And He said to them, "Let us cross over to the other side of the lake." And they launched out. But as they sailed He fell asleep. And a windstorm came down on the lake, and they were filling with water, and were in jeopardy. And they came to Him and awoke Him, saying, "Master, Master, we are perishing!" Then He arose and rebuked the wind and the raging of the water. And they ceased, and there was a calm. But He said to them, "Where is your faith?" And they were afraid, and marveled, saying to one another, "Who can this be? For He commands even the winds and water, and they obey Him!"

LUKE 8:22–25

The sun is rising somewhere right now. Let new thoughts make you a new person. ROBERT H. SCHULLER

THE SYNAGOGUE AT KORAZIN (CHORAZIN), ISRAEL
The Jews of this once thriving town refused to allow Jesus to preach.
Jesus warned them about their disbelief, since mighty miracles had been
performed in their vicinity.

Then He [Jesus] began to rebuke the cities in which most of
His mighty works had been done, because they did not repent:
"Woe to you, Chorazin! Woe to you, Bethsaida! For if the
mighty works which were done in you had been done in Tyre
and Sidon, they would have repented long ago..."

MATTHEW 11:20–21

CHURCH OF THE MIRACLE OF THE SWINE, KURSI, ISRAEL

Kursi is thought to be one of the possible New Testament locations of Gadara (or the Gadarenes). Here Jesus cast multiple demons out of two possessed men, allowing the demons to enter into a herd of pigs. The pigs then ran into the water and drowned. This is certainly an interesting way to get rid of a person's problems! (See page 103 for the full story.)

Therefore, if anyone is in Christ, he is a new creation; old things have passed away; behold, all things have become new. Now all things are of God, who has reconciled us to Himself through Jesus Christ, and has given us the ministry of reconciliation, that is, that God was in Christ reconciling the world to Himself..."

2 CORINTHIANS 5:17–19

RUINS OF GADARA (GADARENES) JORDAN

This town was known as Gadara, one of the ancient Greco-Roman cities of the Decapolis, believed to be the most likely area where the miracle of the swine took place.

From this high point the hills roll down to the Sea of Galilee in the background.

Then they sailed to the country of the Gadarenes, which is opposite Galilee. And when He stepped out on the land, there met Him a certain man from the city who had demons for a long time. And he wore no clothes, nor did he live in a house but in the tombs. When he saw Jesus, he cried out, fell down before Him, and with a loud voice said, "What have I to do with You, Jesus, Son of the Most High God? I beg You, do not torment me!" For He had commanded the unclean spirit to come out of the man. For it had often seized him, and he was kept under guard, bound with chains and shackles; and he broke the bonds and was driven by the demon into the wilderness. Jesus asked him, saying, "What is your name?" And he said, "Legion," because many demons had entered him. And they begged Him that He would not command them to go out into the abyss. Now a herd of many swine was feeding there on the mountain. So they begged Him that He would permit them to enter them. And He permitted them. Then the demons went out of the man and entered the swine, and the herd ran violently down the steep place into the lake and drowned.

LUKE 8:26–33

Let your imagination release your imprisioned possibilities. ROBERT H. SCHULLER **103**

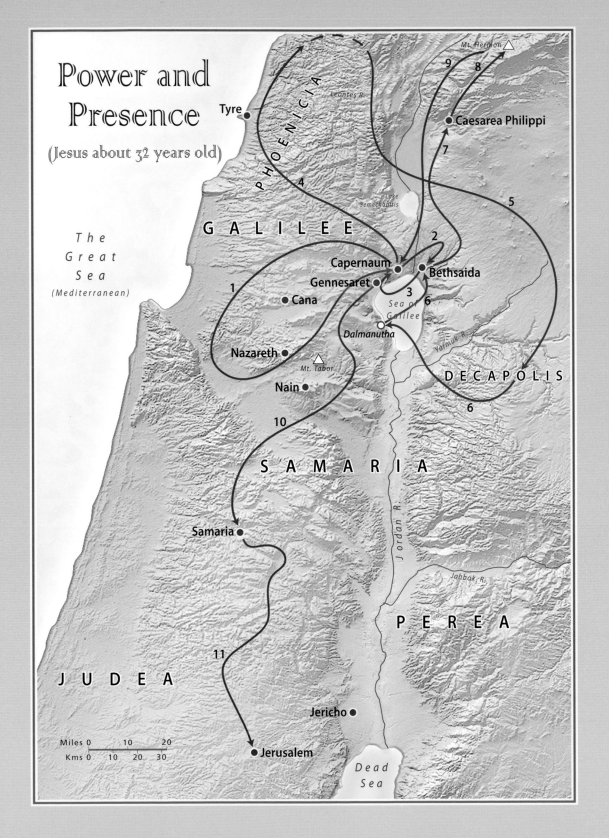

Power and Presence

(Jesus about 32 years old)

The
Great
Sea
(Mediterranean)

PHOENICIA

Tyre

Leontes R.

Mt. Hermon △

9 8

Caesarea Philippi

7

4

Lake
Semechoptis

5

GALILEE

2

Capernaum

Gennesaret Bethsaida

1

3 6

Cana

Sea of
Galilee

Dalmanutha

Nazareth

Yarmuk R.

Mt. Tabor △

DECAPOLIS

Nain

6

10

Jordan R.

SAMARIA

Jabbok R.

Samaria

PEREA

11

JUDEA

Jericho

Miles 0   10   20

Kms 0   10   20   30

Jerusalem

Dead
Sea

KEY

1. Jesus went through the towns of Galilee (Matthew 9:35). He may have been to Mount Tabor at this time where it is possible the transfiguration took place. Luke 9:28–36

2. The miraculous feeding of the five thousand at Bethsaida. Matthew 14:13–21, Mark 6:30–44, Luke 9:10–17, John 6:1–15

3. On the way from Bethsaida to Gennesaret, Jesus walked on the water. Matthew 14:22–34, Mark 6:45–53, John 6:16–24

4. Jesus traveled to Tyre and Sidon and healed the Syrian Phoenician woman. Matthew 15:21–28

5. Jesus left Phoenicia and headed to the Decapolis area, performing miracles on the way. Jesus healed a deaf and dumb man (Mark 7:31–37) and fed the four thousand (Matthew 15:29–39, Mark 8:1–10).

6. From the Decapolis, Jesus went to Dalmanutha, and then by boat to Bethsaida where He healed a blind man. Mark 8:10–26

7. Jesus and His disciples traveled to the villages around Caesarea Philippi where Peter received revelation that Jesus is the Son of God. Matthew 16:13–20, Mark 8:27–30

8. Jesus was transfigured, most likely at Mt Hermon. Matthew 17:1–8, Mark 9:2–8, Luke 9:28–36

9. Jesus returned to Capernaum, the site of the miracle of the coin from the fish's mouth. Matthew 17:24–27

10. Jesus then traveled through Samaria and healed ten lepers. Luke 17:11–19

11. Having arrived in Jerusalem, Jesus healed a blind man at the Pool of Siloam. John 9:1–41

Lines show only general direction and approximate sequence of journeys.

⟶ Jesus' Journey

● Generally accepted or known location

○ Possible location

△ Mountain

I can do all things through Christ who strengthens me.

PHILIPPIANS 4:13

Power and Presence

Problems have come to pass...not to stay.   ROBERT ANTHONY SCHULLER

Jesus was seldom far from the Sea of Galilee, which is a large freshwater lake draining into the Jordan River. Several of His disciples were veterans of the lake, having fished those waters all their lives. The multiplication of loaves and fishes probably occurred on a bluff overlooking the Sea. It is one of the most famous of Jesus' miracles, remarkable both in terms of its largeness and its symbolism: Five loaves and two small fish were miraculously multiplied to feed five thousand people.

It was catering on a massive scale, breaking all the normal "rules" of nature and economics. Amongst its many lessons, it pointed to the fact that Jesus, as the Son of God, was the real supplier of the needs of humanity. Even in our normal lives, when we eat food from the marketplace, we do well when we remember this. All things ultimately come from the Son of God, for "by Him all things were created" (Colossians 1:16). Gradually Jesus' disciples were learning that His presence brought a whole new world of possibilities and insights. Their lives would never again be the same.

105

VIEW OF MT TABOR, ISRAEL

This is believed to be one of the two possible locations for the transfiguration of Jesus.

BASILICA OF THE TRANSFIGURATION,
MT TABOR, ISRAEL

...Jesus took Peter, James, and John his brother, led them up on a high mountain by themselves; and He was transfigured before them. His face shone like the sun, and His clothes became as white as the light. And behold, Moses and Elijah appeared to them, talking with Him... a bright cloud overshadowed them; and suddenly a voice came out of the cloud, saying, "This is My beloved Son, in whom I am well pleased. Hear Him!"

MATTHEW 17:1–5

God's power within me reveals beautiful miracles about me!

ROBERT H. SCHULLER

MILL STONE, CAPERNAUM, ISRAEL

This stone, from the time of Jesus, would have been used to grind wheat for people in the city of Capernaum (where Jesus lived).

[Jesus said] "Therefore do not worry, saying, 'What shall we eat?' or 'What shall we drink?' or 'What shall we wear?'... For your heavenly Father knows that you need all these things. But seek first the kingdom of God and His righteousness, and all these things shall be added to you. Therefore do not worry about tomorrow, for tomorrow will worry about its own things. Sufficient for the day is its own trouble."

MATTHEW 6:31–34

THE SEA OF GALILEE, FROM THE GOLAN HEIGHTS

To the far right of this view, we see the area where the town of Bethsaida was located at the time of Jesus. It was near here that the miracle of the feeding of the five thousand took place.

For every mountain there is a miracle. ROBERT H. SCHULLER **109**

LADY COOKING BREAD, NAZARETH VILLAGE,
NAZARETH, ISRAEL

*And Jesus said to them, "I am the bread of life. He who comes
to Me shall never hunger, and he who believes in Me shall
never thirst. But I said to you that you have seen Me and yet
do not believe... For I have come down from heaven, not to
do My own will, but the will of Him who sent Me. This is the
will of the Father who sent Me, that of all He has given Me I
should lose nothing, but should raise it up at the last day.
And this is the will of Him who sent Me, that everyone who
sees the Son and believes in Him may have everlasting life;
and I will raise him up at the last day."*

JOHN 6:35–40

THE CHURCH OF THE MULTIPLICATION, TABGHA, ISRAEL

The rock under the altar table in this church is traditionally believed to be where Jesus placed five loaves and two fish for blessing. This food then miraculously fed over five thousand people, with plenty left over. Now that is a miracle!

...when Jesus went out He saw a great multitude; and He was moved with compassion for them, and healed their sick. When it was evening, His disciples came to Him, saying, "This is a deserted place, and the hour is already late. Send the multitudes away, that they may go into the villages and buy themselves food." But Jesus said to them, "They do not need to go away. You give them something to eat." And they said to Him, "We have here only five loaves and two fish." He said, "Bring them here to Me." Then He commanded the multitudes to sit down on the grass. And He took the five loaves and the two fish, and looking up to heaven, He blessed and broke and gave the loaves to the disciples; and the disciples gave to the multitudes. So they all ate and were filled, and they took up twelve baskets full of the fragments that remained. Now those who had eaten were about five thousand men, besides women and children.

MATTHEW 14:14–21

FISHERMEN AT TWILIGHT, SEA OF GALILEE, ISRAEL

[Jesus said] *"Ask, and it will be given to you; seek, and you will find; knock, and it will be opened to you."* MATTHEW 7:7

Never let a problem become an excuse. ROBERT H. SCHULLER **113**

Then Jesus went out from there and departed to the region of Tyre and Sidon. And behold, a woman of Canaan came from that region and cried out to Him, saying, "Have mercy on me, O Lord, Son of David! My daughter is severely demon-possessed." But He answered her not a word... Then she came and worshiped Him, saying, "Lord, help me!" But He answered and said, "It is not good to take the children's bread and throw it to the little dogs." And she said, "Yes, Lord, yet even the little dogs eat the crumbs which fall from their masters' table." Then Jesus answered and said to her, "O woman, great is your faith! Let it be to you as you desire." And her daughter was healed from that very hour.

MATTHEW 15:21–28

MAIN STREET, AL BASS ROMAN RUINS, TYRE, LEBANON
Jesus would have walked down this main street while ministering in the area of Tyre.

Life is not a sprint, it's a marathon! ROBERT ANTHONY SCHULLER

THE SEA FORTRESS, SIDON, LEBANON

This crusader fortress was built on Phoenician ruins; in fact some of the stonework from the previous building was used in its construction.

Though the castle would not have been here at the time of Jesus, the harbor itself dates back thousands of years.

SUNSET AT SIDON, LEBANON

A fisherman leaves the safety of the harbor to go fishing overnight in the Mediterranean Sea.

The most tragic waste is the waste of a good idea. ROBERT H. SCHULLER

BANIAS WATERFALL, CAESAREA PHILIPPI, GOLAN HEIGHTS

Jesus and his disciples would almost certainly have seen this beautiful waterfall on their journey to Caesarea Philippi.

It was in this region that the disciple Peter proclaimed, "You are the Christ, the Son of the living God."

God's power makes His possibilities achievable! ROBERT H. SCHULLER

CROSS OF REMEMBRANCE, DALMANUTHA,
SEA OF GALILEE, ISRAEL

This cross marks the traditional spot where Jesus and his
disciples returned after the miracle of the feeding of four
thousand people. (This event is recorded in the Gospel of
Mark, chapter eight.)

*When Jesus came into the region of Caesarea Philippi,
He asked His disciples, saying... "who do you say that
I am?" Simon Peter answered and said, "You are the
Christ, the Son of the living God." Jesus... said to him,
"Blessed are you, Simon Bar-Jonah, for flesh and blood
has not revealed this to you, but My Father who is in
heaven."*

MATTHEW 16:13–17

As He [Jesus] prayed, the appearance of His face was altered, and His robe became white and glistening. And behold, two men talked with Him, who were Moses and Elijah, who appeared in glory and spoke of His decease which He was about to accomplish at Jerusalem.

LUKE 9:29–31

MOUNT HERMON IN WINTER, GOLAN HEIGHTS
Mount Hermon is one of the possible sites of Jesus' Transfiguration. (Mount Tabor on pages 106–107 is the other.)

Summer, winter, spring and fall, God is in control of all.   ROBERT H.SCHULLER

FISHERMEN ON THE SEA OF GALILEE, ISRAEL

SAINT PETER'S FISH, SEA OF GALILEE, ISRAEL

To pay the temple tax, Jesus instructed Peter to go and catch a fish, which would have money in its mouth. This happened, just as Jesus predicted. Jesus obviously had a sense of humor. What an interesting way to pay taxes—it makes you want to take up fishing!

When they had come to Capernaum, those who received the temple tax came to Peter and said, "Does your Teacher not pay the temple tax?" He said, "Yes." And when he had come into the house, Jesus anticipated him, saying... From whom do the kings of the earth take customs or taxes, from their sons or from strangers?" Peter said to Him, "From strangers." Jesus said to him, "Then the sons are free. Nevertheless, lest we offend them, go to the sea, cast in a hook, and take the fish that comes up first. And when you have opened its mouth, you will find a piece of money; take that and give it to them for Me and you."

MATTHEW 17:24–27

Add up your joys—never count your sorrows.   ROBERT H. SCHULLER   **123**

Now it happened as He went to Jerusalem that He passed through the midst of Samaria and Galilee. Then as He entered a certain village, there met Him ten men who were lepers, who stood afar off. And they lifted up their voices and said, "Jesus, Master, have mercy on us!" So when He saw them, He said to them, "Go, show yourselves to the priests." And so it was that as they went, they were cleansed. And one of them, when he saw that he was healed, returned, and with a loud voice glorified God, and fell down on his face at His feet, giving Him thanks...

LUKE 17:11–16

ROMAN RUINS, ANCIENT CITY OF SEBASTE, SAMARIA, PALESTINE
Jesus healed ten lepers in this area of Samaria.

No one emerges from a problem untouched by tough times. But you have managed to turn your hurts into halos and your scars into stars!

POOL OF SILOAM, JERUSALEM
At the Pool of Siloam, Jesus healed a man born blind.

I must work the works of Him who sent Me while it is day; the night is coming when no one can work. As long as I am in the world, I am the light of the world." When He had said these things, He spat on the ground and made clay with the saliva; and He anointed the eyes of the blind man with the clay. And He said to him, "Go, wash in the pool of Siloam" ... So he went and washed, and came back seeing.

JOHN 9:4–7

When it looks like you've exhausted all possibilities. . . remember this: you haven't! ROBERT H. SCHULLER

SUNRISE OVER MOUNT ZION, JERUSALEM

[Jesus said] "...in Me you may have peace. In the world you will have tribulation; but be of good cheer, I have overcome the world." JOHN 16:33

Let your hopes, not your hurts, shape your future. ROBERT H. SCHULLER **129**

Jesus' Last Months

(Jesus about 33 years old)

SAMARIA

Jordan R.

Jabbok R.

PEREA

JUDEA

● Ephraim

3

● Jericho

4

○ Bethany (Bethabara)

5

6

Jerusalem ● 7

● Bethany

1

Dead Sea

Miles 0   10
Kms 0   10

KEY

1. Jesus traveled from Bethabara to Bethany near Jerusalem and raised Lazarus from the dead. John 11:1–46

2. Jesus withdrew to Ephraim in the countryside. John 11:54

3. Jesus crossed the Jordan into Perea, healed a crippled woman (Luke 13:10–13) and blessed the children (Luke 18:15–17).

4. Jesus traveled to Jericho and transformed Zacchaeus' life. Luke 19:1–10

5. Jesus healed two blind men outside Jericho on the road to Bethany. Matthew 20:29–34,

6. Mary anointed the feet of Jesus in Bethany. John 12:1–8

7.Jesus made his triumphal entry into Jerusalem on the back of a donkey. Matthew 21:1–11, Mark 11:1–11, Luke 19:28–44, John 12:12–16

Lines show only general direction and approximate sequence of journeys.

⟶ Jesus' Journey

● Generally accepted or known location

○ Possible location

MOSAIC OF LAZARUS COMING OUT OF THE TOMB,
CHURCH OF SAINT LAZARUS, BETHANY, PALESTINE

[Jesus said] "...the hour is coming, and now is,
when the dead will hear the voice of the Son of God; and those who hear will live."

JOHN 5:25

Jesus' Last Months

Success without conflict is unrealistic.   ROBERT H. SCHULLER

Followers and enemies walked with Jesus almost every day. As His influence grew, so did the desperation of those anxious to silence Him. Even when Jesus raised Lazarus from the dead—an astounding miracle by any standards—the response was mixed. Many put their faith in Jesus. But others began to plot His death.

For weeks, Jesus moved steadily toward Jerusalem. He had traveled there before, but now His journey had the look and feel of a final visit. He was moving in that direction spiritually as well as geographically. When Jesus told His disciples what would happen in Jerusalem, they were confused. They resisted the idea of Jesus' death. How could He be the Messiah and yet die? How could He be king and not live to reign?

Jesus gave them clues, even clear answers, but they remained unconvinced, unprepared, and troubled. Although the ominous future made them fear for their own lives, they continued to walk with Jesus. They didn't abandon Him—yet. Thomas seems to have expressed their inner turmoil with a unique sense of resigned faith: "Let us also go, that we may die with Him" (John 11:16).

THE DEAD SEA, ISRAEL   Jesus would have seen the Dead Sea, as it is not far from the Bethany (Bethabara) region where Jesus spent time.

The Dead Sea, 1296 feet (395 meters) below sea level, is the lowest point on the surface of the earth. The Jordan River flows into this lake but ends here, since the lake has no outlet.

...though I walk through the valley of the shadow of death, I will fear no evil; for You are with me... PSALM 23:4

Impossible situations can become possible miracles. ROBERT H. SCHULLER **133**

SHEPHERD, JERICHO TO JERUSALEM ROAD, PALESTINE

A shepherd grazes his sheep on the route most likely traveled by Jesus on his way to Bethany from Jericho. In the days of Jesus, these hills were often used by robbers trying to ambush unaware travelers. Maybe this knowledge inspired Jesus' parable of the Good Samaritan. Many people believe this story was based on a true event which occurred close to this location.

[A man]...wanting to justify himself, said to Jesus, "And who is my neighbor?"... Jesus answered and said: "A certain man went down from Jerusalem to Jericho, and fell among thieves, who stripped him of his clothing, wounded him, and departed, leaving him half dead. Now by chance a certain priest came down that road. And when he saw him, he passed by on the other side. Likewise a Levite, when he arrived at the place, came and looked, and passed by on the other side. But a certain Samaritan, as he journeyed, came where he was. And when he saw him, he had compassion. So he went to him and bandaged his wounds, pouring on oil and wine; and he set him on his own animal, brought him to an inn, and took care of him. On the next day, when he departed, he took out two denarii, gave them to the innkeeper, and said to him, 'Take care of him; and whatever more you spend, when I come again, I will repay you.' So which of these three do you think was neighbor to him who fell among the thieves?" And he said, "He who showed mercy on him." Then Jesus said to him, "Go and do likewise."

LUKE 10:29–37

God can keep you focused on your goals, despite every injustice in your path.

ROBERT H. SCHULLER

MOSAIC OF MARY AND MARTHA GREETING JESUS, CHURCH OF
SAINT LAZARUS, BETHANY, PALESTINE

Hearing of Lazarus' death, Jesus came to Bethany. The sisters of Lazarus—Mary and
Martha—met Jesus on the way. But they felt Jesus' return was too late: Lazarus was dead.
Jesus, knowing God's will, raised Lazarus from death. Jesus is the Son of the *living* God!

TOMB OF LAZARUS, BETHANY, PALESTINE

This is the tomb where, it is believed, Jesus raised Lazarus from the dead.

"Our friend Lazarus sleeps, but I go that I may wake him up."
Then His disciples said, "Lord, if he sleeps he will get well."
However, Jesus spoke of his death... Jesus said to them plainly,
"Lazarus is dead... Nevertheless let us go to him." ...Martha
[sister of Lazarus], as soon as she heard that Jesus was coming,
went and met Him... Jesus said to her, "I am the resurrection
and the life. He who believes in Me, though he may die, he shall
live. And whoever lives and believes in Me shall never die.
Do you believe this?" She said to Him, "Yes, Lord, I believe
that You are the Christ, the Son of God, who is to come into
the world."... [Martha] went her way and secretly called Mary
[Her sister]... when Mary came where Jesus was, and saw
Him, she fell down at His feet... when Jesus saw her weeping...
He groaned in the spirit and was troubled. And He said,
"Where have you laid him?"... [Jesus] came to the tomb. It was
a cave, and a stone lay against it. Jesus said, "Take away the
stone." Martha... said to Him, "Lord, by this time there is a
stench, for he has been dead four days." Jesus said to her, "Did I
not say to you that if you would believe you would see the
glory of God?" Then they took away the stone... And Jesus
lifted up His eyes and said, "Father, I thank You that You
have heard Me. And I know that You always hear Me... I
said this, that they may believe that You sent Me." Now when
He had said these things, He cried with a loud voice,
"Lazarus, come forth!" And he who had died came out bound
hand and foot with graveclothes, and his face was wrapped
with a cloth. Jesus said to them, "Loose him, and let him go."

JOHN 11:11–44

SHEPHERDS ON THE ROAD TO EPHRAIM (TAYBA), PALESTINE

After the miracle of raising Lazarus from the dead, many believed in Jesus. The Jewish chief priest and the Pharisees were not happy. They gave a command, that if anyone knew where Jesus was they should report it, so they could seize Him. Knowing this, Jesus retreated into the countryside, to a city called Ephraim.

BYZANTINE CHURCH, EPHRAIM (TAYBA), PALESTINE
This church was built to honor the time Jesus spent in the area of Ephraim.

Therefore Jesus no longer walked openly among the Jews, but went... into the country near the wilderness, to a city called Ephraim, and there remained with His disciples.

JOHN 11:54

CARDO MAXIMUS, JERASH, JORDAN   This is the main avenue of one of the Decapolis cities that Jesus almost certainly visited.

Turn your stumbling blocks into stepping stones. ROBERT H. SCHULLER

141

THE ZACCHAEUS TREE, JERICHO, PALESTINE

This tree is said to be over two thousand years old. Perhaps it was the very tree that Zacchaeus climbed when Jesus visited Jericho?

...Jesus entered and passed through Jericho... there was a man named Zacchaeus who was a chief tax collector, and he was rich... he sought to see who Jesus was, but could not because of the crowd, for he was of short stature. So he ran ahead and climbed up into a sycamore tree to see Him, for He was going to pass that way... when Jesus came to the place, He looked up and saw him, and said to him, "Zacchaeus, make haste and come down, for today I must stay at your house." So he made haste and came down, and received Him joyfully. But when they saw it, they all complained, saying, "He has gone to be a guest with a man who is a sinner." Then Zacchaeus stood and said to the Lord, "Look, Lord, I give half of my goods to the poor; and if I have taken anything from anyone by false accusation, I restore fourfold." And Jesus said to him, "Today salvation has come to this house... for the Son of Man has come to seek and to save that which was lost."

LUKE 19:1–10

Inch by inch anything's a cinch! ROBERT H. SCHULLER

143

HEROD THE GREAT'S WINTER PALACE, WADI QELT, JERICHO, PALESTINE

Jesus would have seen this palace just outside Jericho on His way to Jerusalem. His healing of two blind men would presumably have occurred close by.

...as they went out of Jericho, a great multitude followed Him. And behold, two blind men sitting by the road, when they heard that Jesus was passing by, cried out, saying, "Have mercy on us, O Lord, Son of David!" Then the multitude warned them that they should be quiet; but they cried out all the more, saying, "Have mercy on us, O Lord, Son of David!" So Jesus stood still and called them, and said, "What do you want Me to do for you?" They said to Him, "Lord, that our eyes may be opened." So Jesus had compassion and touched their eyes. And immediately their eyes received sight, and they followed Him.

MATTHEW 20:29–34

God believes in you and he can't be wrong. ROBERT H. SCHULLER **145**

THE HILLS OUTSIDE JERICHO, PALESTINE

"The LORD bless you and keep you;
The LORD make His face shine upon you,
And be gracious to you;
The LORD lift up His countenance upon you,
And give you peace."

NUMBERS 6:24–26

BOY WITH CAMEL, JUDEAN DESERT, BETWEEN JERICHO AND JERUSALEM, PALESTINE

Building boys is better than mending men. ROBERT H. SCHULLER

WHITE DOVE, WESTERN WALL (WAILING WALL),
JERUSALEM, ISRAEL

A white dove is symbolic of peace. How appropriate that it rests on the
Wailing Wall, a place of prayer. Jesus gave His life for us that we may have
peace with God, and we also should pray for the "peace of Jerusalem".

FRESCO OF JESUS' TRIUMPHAL ENTRY INTO JERUSALEM,
SANCTUARY OF BETHPHAGE, PALESTINE

For God so loved the world that He gave His only begotten Son,
that whoever believes in Him should not perish but have everlasting life.

JOHN 3:16

Jesus' Last Days

Love isn't love until you give it away.   ROBERT H. SCHULLER

The air that morning seemed shot through with anticipation. Pilgrims on their way to Jerusalem for the Passover knew they would be in the city by nightfall. For many of them, this would be their first time in David's City. The traditional "Psalms of Ascent" were on everyone's lips. People were in a mood to praise God!

Then news spread through the crowd that Jesus—the prophet, healer and (some said) Messiah—was among them. Mounted on a young donkey, Jesus reminded many of the ancient tradition of kings riding on colts when they approached the great city in peace. The sign represented humility more than royalty. And that's why this entrance into Jerusalem was all the more triumphant; because Jesus had a victory of a different kind in mind—one that would require the ultimate sacrifice.

As we follow Jesus through Jerusalem, we soon realize that He walked there in our place, for our benefit. He took the steps that led to the cross on our behalf. Isaiah described this process centuries earlier when he wrote, "But He was wounded for our transgressions, He was bruised for our iniquities; the chastisement for our peace was upon Him, and by His stripes we are healed" (Isaiah 53:5).

...when they drew near Jerusalem, and came to Bethphage... Jesus sent two disciples, saying to them, "Go into the village opposite you, and immediately you will find a donkey tied, and a colt with her. Loose them and bring them to Me. And if anyone says anything to you, you shall say, 'The Lord has need of them,' and immediately he will send them." All this was done that it might be fulfilled which was spoken by the prophet, saying: "Tell the daughter of Zion [Jerusalem], 'Behold, your King is coming to you, lowly, and sitting on a donkey, a colt, the foal of a donkey.'"

MATTHEW 21:1–5

EXTERIOR, SANCTUARY OF BETHPHAGE, PALESTINE
Outside the Sanctuary of Bethphage, a local stands with what he calls a 'Jerusalem Taxi'.
Many, it seems, still like riding on a donkey, just as Jesus did when He entered Jerusalem.

They brought the donkey and the colt, laid their
clothes on them, and set Him on them. And a very
great multitude spread their clothes on the road;
others cut down branches from the trees and spread
them on the road. Then the multitudes who went
before and those who followed cried out, saying:
"Hosanna [Praise God] to the Son of David!
'Blessed is He who comes in the name of the LORD!'
Hosanna in the highest!"

MATTHEW 21:7–9

INTERIOR, SANCTUARY OF BETHPHAGE, PALESTINE
In this sanctuary there is a stone (inside the fenced area) said to bear the imprint of Jesus'
foot as he mounted the young donkey. It was from this village that Jesus rode into Jerusalem.

Then, as He was now drawing near the descent of the Mount of Olives, the whole multitude of the disciples began to rejoice and praise God with a loud voice for all the mighty works they had seen, saying: " 'Blessed is the King who comes in the name of the LORD!' Peace in heaven and glory in the highest!"

LUKE 19:37–38

JESUS' TRIUMPHAL ENTRY INTO JERUSALEM
This is the road Jesus would have taken into Jerusalem from the Mount of Olives.

WESTERN WALL (WAILING WALL), JERUSALEM
The Wailing Wall is a retaining wall which helps form the plateau area
(the Temple Mount) on which the temple stood at the time of Jesus.

Pray for the peace of Jerusalem: "May they prosper who love you."

PSALM 122:6

Total peace will only come from total commitment. ROBERT H. SCHULLER **153**

KIDRON VALLEY, JERUSALEM

Jesus walked through this valley on His way to the Last Supper and on His way to pray in the Garden of Gethsemane.

When God sees a breech he builds a bridge. ROBERT H. SCHULLER

...the disciples came to Jesus, saying to Him, "Where do You want us to prepare for You to eat the Passover?" And He said, "Go into the city to a certain man, and say to him, 'The Teacher says, "My time is at hand; I will keep the Passover at your house with My disciples." ' " So the disciples did as Jesus had directed them; and they prepared the Passover. When evening had come, He sat down with the twelve. Now as they were eating, He said, "Assuredly, I say to you, one of you will betray Me."... Then Judas, who was betraying Him, answered and said, "Rabbi, is it I?" He [Jesus] said to him, "You have said it."

MATTHEW 26:17–25

THE UPPER ROOM, MOUNT ZION, JERUSALEM
This room (a Fourteenth Century renovation) is believed to be where Jesus and His disciples celebrated the Last Supper and where Jesus washed His disciples' feet.

[Jesus said] In this manner, therefore, pray:
Our Father in heaven,
Hallowed be Your name.
Your kingdom come.
Your will be done
On earth as it is in heaven.
Give us this day our daily bread.
And forgive us our debts,
As we forgive our debtors.
And do not lead us into temptation,
But deliver us from the evil one.
For Yours is the kingdom
and the power and the glory forever.
Amen.

MATTHEW 6:9–13

And as they were eating, Jesus took bread, blessed and
broke it, and gave it to the disciples and said, "Take,
eat; this is My body." Then He took the cup, and gave
thanks, and gave it to them, saying, "Drink from it,
all of you. For this is My blood of the new covenant,
which is shed for many for the remission of sins. But
I say to you, I will not drink of this fruit of the vine
from now on until that day when I drink it new with
you in My Father's kingdom."

MATTHEW 26:26–29

TRADITIONAL FOOD LAID OUT, AS IN THE DAYS OF JESUS

I will live today as a new person because Jesus forgives me and gives me a new life, new love and enthusiasm. ROBERT H. SCHULLER **157**

Then Jesus came with them to a place called Gethsemane, and said to the disciples, "Sit here while I go and pray over there." And He took with Him Peter and the two sons of Zebedee, and He began to be sorrowful and deeply distressed. Then He said to them, "My soul is exceedingly sorrowful, even to death. Stay here and watch with Me." He went a little farther and fell on His face, and prayed...

MATTHEW 26:36–39

THE GARDEN OF GETHSEMANE, JERUSALEM
Historians are in general agreement that this is the site of the original Garden of Gethsemane.
Remarkably, some of these olive trees are reported to be from the time of Jesus.

Love blooms when we love each other. ROBERT H. SCHULLER

SILVER COINS FROM THE TIME OF JESUS
These silver coins are similar to the ones paid to Judas for betraying Jesus.

Then one of the twelve, called Judas Iscariot, went to the chief priests and said, "What are you willing to give me if I deliver Him [Jesus] to you?" And they counted out to him thirty pieces of silver.

MATTHEW 26:14–15

PILLAR OF THE KISS, GARDEN OF GETHSEMANE, JERUSALEM
This pillar marks the traditional place where Judas betrayed Jesus with a kiss.

...and he who was called Judas, one of the twelve, went before them and drew near to Jesus to kiss Him. But Jesus said to him, "Judas, are you betraying the Son of Man with a kiss?"

LUKE 22:47–48

THE BASILICA OF THE AGONY. JERUSALEM

This church in the Garden of Gethsemane is believed to be where Jesus prayed. The rock in the foreground, called the Rock of the Agony, is thought to be the exact spot of His prayer.

...He [Jesus] knelt down and prayed, saying, "Father, if it is Your will, take this cup away from Me; nevertheless not My will, but Yours, be done." Then an angel appeared to Him from heaven, strengthening Him. And being in agony, He prayed more earnestly. Then His sweat became like great drops of blood falling down to the ground.

LUKE 22:41–44

EXTERIOR. CHURCH OF THE HOLY ARCHANGEL. JERUSALEM

After Jesus was arrested, He was taken to the house of Annas, the father-in-law of the high priest. This church marks the location where the dwelling is believed to have stood.

Then the detachment of troops and the captain and the officers of the Jews arrested Jesus and bound Him. And they led Him away to Annas first, for he was the father-in-law of Caiaphas who was high priest that year. Now it was Caiaphas who advised the Jews that it was expedient that one man should die for the people.

JOHN 18:12–14

INTERIOR, CHURCH OF THE HOLY ARCHANGEL, JERUSALEM

According to Armenian Christian tradition, this small chapel inside the church is believed to mark the place where Jesus was held while in Annas' house. It was from here that Jesus was then taken to the house of the high priest, Caiaphas.

And the high priest arose and said to Him, "Do You answer nothing? What is it these men testify against You?" But Jesus kept silent. And the high priest answered and said to Him, "I put You under oath by the living God: Tell us if You are the Christ, the Son of God!" Jesus said to him, " It is as you said. Nevertheless, I say to you, hereafter you will see the Son of Man sitting at the right hand of the Power, and coming on the clouds of heaven." Then the high priest tore his clothes, saying, "He has spoken blasphemy! What further need do we have of witnesses? Look, now you have heard His blasphemy! What do you think?" They answered and said, "He is deserving of death."

MATTHEW 26:62–66

STEPS TO CAIAPHAS' HOUSE, KIDRON VALLEY, JERUSALEM

These ancient steps date from before the time of Jesus. This is the most probable way Jesus was led to Caiaphas' house.

God's care will carry you so you can carry others! ROBERT H. SCHULLER

THE VIA DOLOROSA, JERUSALEM

The Via Dolorosa (Way of Sorrow or Way of the Cross) is Christendom's most sacred pilgrimage route. It follows the path believed taken by Jesus from Pilate's judgment to the place of crucifixion.

Then they led Jesus from Caiaphas to the Praetorium... [to Pilate, and he said to Jesus] "...Your own nation and the chief priests have delivered You to me. What have You done?" Jesus answered, "My kingdom is not of this world..." Pilate therefore said to Him, "Are You a king then?" Jesus answered, "You say rightly that I am a king. For this cause I was born, and for this cause I have come into the world, that I should bear witness to the truth. Everyone who is of the truth hears My voice." Pilate said to Him, "What is truth?" And... he went out again to the Jews, and said to them, "I find no fault in Him at all."

JOHN 18:28–38

Now at the feast the governor was accustomed to releasing... one prisoner... And at that time they had a notorious prisoner called Barabbas. Therefore, when they had gathered together, Pilate said to them, "Whom do you want me to release to you? Barabbas, or Jesus who is called Christ?" For he knew that they had handed Him over because of envy... But the chief priests and elders persuaded the multitudes that they should ask for Barabbas and destroy Jesus... [Pilate] said to them, "Which of the two do you want me to release to you?" They said, "Barabbas!" Pilate said to them, "What then shall I do with Jesus who is called Christ?" They all said to him, "Let Him be crucified!"

MATTHEW 27:15–22

THE PRISON OF CHRIST,
GREEK ORTHODOX CHURCH, JERUSALEM
The underground rooms of the Greek Orthodox Church are said to have
been the prison where Jesus was held, tried and whipped.

TWILIGHT OVER JERUSALEM

[Jesus said] "I am the way, the truth, and the life..." JOHN 14:6

PAINTED SCULPTURE, CHAPEL OF THE CONDEMNATION, JERUSALEM

This is My commandment, that you love one another as I have loved you.
Greater love has no one than this, than to lay down one's life for his friends.

JOHN 15:12–13

Jesus' Steps to the Cross

Love is a choice   ROBERT ANTHONY SCHULLER

Jesus' final steps were as purposeful as they were agonizing. He dragged His cross and the weight of human sin through Jerusalem and up the hill called "The Skull". Scripture and tradition mention several stops along the way. Many Christians from traditional backgrounds now commemorate these various stages as the fourteen "Stations of the Cross". Each stage has its own traditional site, venerated through the centuries. For many pilgrims, these help focus heart and mind on events of enormous significance—as if history itself was slowed to a walking pace on this momentous day.

But the crucial fact is that Jesus never really stopped. He walked all the way to the place of crucifixion, allowing people like us to nail him to the timbers. There was an awe-inspiring deliberateness about it all. The nails, it has been said, didn't hold him in place; his love did.

Betrayal, abandonment, injustice and abuse filled Jesus' last hours. He walked His final steps so that we would never have to run the same gauntlet. He took our place. The identification with us as humans that began in Mary's womb reached its deepest significance when He identified with us as sinners on the cross. Once that purpose had been accomplished, His work was completed. No wonder He cried from the cross, "It is finished!"

FIRST STATION OF THE CROSS (JESUS IS CONDEMNED TO DEATH), ECCE HOMO ARCH, JERUSALEM
According to tradition, this is the spot where Pilate delivered Jesus to the crowd for crucifixion and proclaimed, "Ecce homo"—Behold the Man.

...Pilate took Jesus and scourged Him. And the soldiers twisted a crown of thorns and put it on His head, and they put on Him a purple robe. Then they said, "Hail, King of the Jews!" And they struck Him with their hands. Pilate then went out again, and said to them, "Behold, I am bringing Him out to you, that you may know that I find no fault in Him." Then Jesus came out, wearing the crown of thorns and the purple robe. And Pilate said to them, "Behold the Man!"

JOHN 19:1–5

SECOND STATION OF THE CROSS (JESUS CARRIES HIS
CROSS), THE LITHOSTROTOS, JERUSALEM
These paving stones are in the courtyard of the Antonio Fortress. On
this pavement Jesus took up His cross and began the grueling trek
to His crucifixion.

*...Pilate said to Him, "...Do You not know that I have power
to crucify You, and power to release You?" Jesus answered,
"You could have no power at all against Me unless it had been
given you from above..."*

JOHN 19:10–11

FOURTH STATION OF THE CROSS (JESUS MEETS
HIS MOTHER MARY), VIA DOLOROSA, JERUSALEM
Though it is not stated in the Bible, tradition holds that this is the
location where Mary embraced her Son. Imagine a mother having to
watch her child go through such torment—yet in her heart she knew
it was the path He had chosen.

THIRD STATION OF THE CROSS (JESUS FALLS FOR
THE FIRST TIME), VIA DOLOROSA, JERUSALEM
This location is marked by a small chapel on the Via Dolorosa. Pilgrims
pause to reflect in the presence of a beautiful marble sculpture.

THE VIA DOLOROSA, JERUSALEM

But He was wounded for our transgressions,
He was bruised for our iniquities;
The chastisement for our peace was upon Him,
And by His stripes we are healed.
All we like sheep have gone astray;
We have turned, every one, to his own way;
And the LORD has laid on Him the iniquity of us all.

ISAIAH 53:5–6

The path of humility is the path to glory. ROBERT H. SCHULLER **173**

SIXTH STATION OF THE CROSS (VERONICA WIPES THE FACE OF JESUS), VIA DOLOROSA, JERUSALEM
According to tradition, a woman called Veronica had compassion on Jesus as He walked with His cross. She dabbed His face with a cloth, leaving an outline of His features on the fabric. It is claimed this cloth is the one now kept at Saint Peters Church in Rome.

FIFTH STATION OF THE CROSS (SIMON OF CYRENE HELPS JESUS CARRY HIS CROSS), VIA DOLOROSA, JERUSALEM

Now as they came out, they found a man of Cyrene, Simon by name. Him they compelled to bear His cross.

MATTHEW 27:32

SEVENTH STATION OF THE CROSS (JESUS' SECOND FALL),
VIA DOLOROSA, JERUSALEM

We cannot be sure how many times, or exactly where, Jesus fell, but these
sites from early Christian tradition give us an opportunity to reflect upon
the agonies Jesus went through. Still, after all that Jesus endured, He said of
the perpetrators, "Father, forgive them, for they do not know what they do"
(Luke 23:34). Now that is forgiveness.

Trying times are times to triumph. ROBERT H. SCHULLER **175**

EIGHTH STATION OF THE CROSS (JESUS CONSOLES THE WOMEN OF JERUSALEM), VIA DOLOROSA, JERUSALEM

This Latin cross, along with an inscription reading "Jesus Christ is Victorious", marks the spot on the Via Dolorosa where it is believed Jesus spoke to a group of mourning women.

[Turning to them Jesus said] "Daughters of Jerusalem, do not weep for Me, but weep for yourselves and for your children."

LUKE 23:28

NINTH STATION OF THE CROSS (JESUS FALLS THE THIRD TIME), VIA DOLOROSA, JERUSALEM

A column on the right hand side of this doorway is believed to mark the site of Jesus' third fall. From here, Jesus would have been close enough to see the place of His imminent crucifixion.

TENTH STATION OF THE CROSS (JESUS STRIPPED OF HIS GARMENTS), CHURCH OF THE HOLY SEPULCHER, JERUSALEM

A stairway of stone leads to this small chapel inside the Church of the Holy Sepulcher. This chapel marks the spot where it is believed Jesus was stripped of his clothes.

...they divided His garments and cast lots. And the people stood looking on...

LUKE 23:34–35

ELEVENTH STATION OF THE CROSS (JESUS IS NAILED TO THE CROSS), CHURCH OF THE HOLY SEPULCHER, JERUSALEM

Magnificent mosaics grace the site where it is believed Jesus was nailed to the cross.

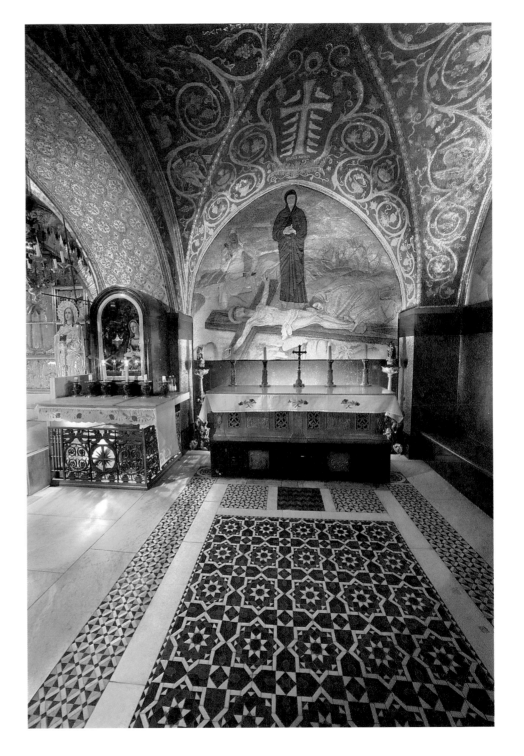

TWELFTH STATION OF THE CROSS (JESUS DIES ON THE CROSS), CHURCH OF THE HOLY SEPULCHER, JERUSALEM

This church is believed to be built on the site of Golgotha (Calvary). The photo shows the altar built over the place where Jesus was supposedly crucified. The rock seen in the glass cases is believed to be the original rock of Golgotha, where the thieves were crucified on either side of Jesus. According to tradition, a large crack in this rock was caused by the miraculous weather accompanying Jesus' death.

Then one of the criminals who were hanged blasphemed Him, saying, "If You are the Christ, save Yourself and us." But the other, answering, rebuked him, saying, "Do you not even fear God, seeing you are under the same condemnation? And we indeed justly, for we receive the due reward of our deeds; but this Man has done nothing wrong." Then he said to Jesus, "Lord, remember me when You come into Your kingdom." And Jesus said to him, "Assuredly, I say to you, today you will be with Me in Paradise"... And when Jesus had cried out with a loud voice, He said, "Father, 'into Your hands I commit My spirit.' " Having said this, He breathed His last. So when the centurion saw what had happened, he glorified God, saying, "Certainly this was a righteous Man!"

LUKE 23:39–47

Grace to you and peace from God the Father and our Lord Jesus Christ, who gave Himself for our sins, that He might deliver us from this present evil age, according to the will of our God and Father...

GALATIANS 1:3–4

THIRTEENTH STATION OF THE CROSS (JESUS IS TAKEN DOWN FROM THE CROSS), CHURCH OF THE HOLY SEPULCHER, JERUSALEM

This altar, with its large stone slab, marks the spot where it is believed Jesus' body was placed after He was taken down from the cross. The stone (called the Stone of Unction or Anointing) is also believed to be the place where Jesus' body was prepared for burial with a blend of myrrh, aloe and aromatic oils.

FOURTEENTH STATION OF THE CROSS (JESUS IS PLACED IN THE TOMB). CHURCH OF THE HOLY SEPULCHER. JERUSALEM

The Holy Sepulcher (that is, Jesus' burial chamber or tomb) is said to lie within this small chapel in the center of the rotunda of the Church of the Holy Sepulcher. This tomb was originally a cave hewn out of rock; the rotunda was built over and around the tomb to preserve and protect it.

FOURTEENTH STATION OF THE CROSS, CHURCH OF THE HOLY
SEPULCHER, JERUSALEM

As the traditional burial place of Jesus, the Church of the Holy Sepulcher is one
of the most holy sites in Christendom. The tomb itself is said to be covered by a
smooth marble slab. In spite of the enormous changes since the time of Christ,
this place retains an overwhelming sense of presence.

Today's impossibilities are tomorrow's miracles. ROBERT H. SCHULLER **181**

THE GARDEN TOMB, JERUSALEM

Many Christians believe the Garden Tomb area is the actual site of Jesus' burial (rather than the site beneath the Church of the Holy Sepulcher).

Some evidence supports their claim and certainly a great sense of peace and holiness permeates this location.

GOLGOTHA, JERUSALEM

This area many believe to be the location of Golgotha—the Hebrew word for 'Place of the Skull'—where Jesus was crucified. The cliff or knoll indeed resembles a skull, and this area fits the Biblical description. It is outside the gates, close to the city and near the Garden Tomb where many believe Jesus was buried.

And He, bearing His cross, went out to a place called the Place of a Skull, which is called in Hebrew, Golgotha, where they crucified Him, and two others with Him, one on either side, and Jesus in the center.

JOHN 19:17–18

You can live without something, if you have someone to live for.   ROBERT H. SCHULLER

LIGHTNING OVER JERUSALEM

In the presence of hope—faith is born. In the presence of faith—love becomes a possibility. In the presence of love—miracles happen! ROBERT H. SCHULLER

THE WESTERN WALL (WAILING WALL),
LOOKING TOWARDS THE MOUNT OF OLIVES,
JERUSALEM

[Jesus said] "Come to Me, all you who labor
and are heavy laden, and I will give you rest."

MOSAIC, MOUNT TABOR, ISRAEL

[Jesus said] "I am He who lives, and was dead, and behold, I am alive forevermore..."

REVELATION 1:18

Jesus' Victory over Death

Turn your scars into stars! ROBERT H. SCHULLER

Imagine a Sunday morning, centuries ago. A vacancy sign goes up outside a tomb in Jerusalem. It was something that never usually happens—in Jerusalem or anywhere else. Tombs are either empty or full—never vacant. It would mean that someone had occupied the space and then had vacated it. Dead people don't vacate!

But Jesus did. Not because He was dead; but because He left death and then the grave behind. He arose! He was seen walking, talking and eating. Those who had seen His hands and feet nailed to the cross thought it was over, that Jesus would never walk again. His death had confirmed their fears. But they had forgotten Jesus had foreseen their confusion and had encouraged them to be patient. These early followers were too afraid to wait—too ashamed to wait—too devastated to wait. So they were surprised! In fact, they were overwhelmed by His resurrection.

Jesus rose physically. That means, among other things, that He had more walking to do, more steps to take. The promise of the resurrection includes this amazing thought: we will spend eternity walking where Jesus walks. And He will walk with us.

THE GARDEN TOMB, JERUSALEM

The tomb of Jesus had a big stone that rolled over the entry. The grave pictured still
has a track along which such a stone would have rolled—thus further evidence that
this may really be the tomb of Jesus. According to the Scriptures, the stone was
rolled away when Jesus rose from the dead. Here, a modern door on the tomb sums it
up: He is not here—for He is risen.

*...very early in the morning, they [women who
followed Jesus] came to the tomb... But they found
the stone rolled away from the tomb. Then they went
in and did not find the body of the Lord Jesus. And
it happened, as they were greatly perplexed about
this, that behold, two men stood by them in shining
garments... they said to them, "Why do you seek the
living among the dead? He is not here, but is risen!
Remember how He spoke to you when He was still in
Galilee, saying, 'The Son of Man must be delivered
into the hands of sinful men, and be crucified, and
the third day rise again.' " And they remembered
His words. Then they returned from the tomb and
told all these things to the eleven and to all the rest.*

LUKE 24:1–9

INTERIOR, THE GARDEN TOMB, JERUSALEM

TRANQUIL GARDENS, THE GARDEN TOMB, JERUSALEM

[Jesus said] "...If anyone loves Me, he will keep My word; and My Father will love him, and We will come to him and make Our home with him... I have spoken to you while being present with you. But the Helper, the Holy Spirit, whom the Father will send in My name, He will teach you all things, and bring to your remembrance all things that I said to you. Peace I leave with you, My peace I give to you; not as the world gives do I give to you. Let not your heart be troubled, neither let it be afraid. You have heard Me say to you, 'I am going away and coming back to you.' If you loved Me, you would rejoice because I said, 'I am going to the Father,' for My Father is greater than I."

JOHN 14:23–28

TEMPLE AT EMMAUS, AYALON VALLEY, ISRAEL
It was at Emmaus that the risen Jesus appeared to two of His followers,
Simeon and Cleopas. Jesus dined with them in Cleopas' house. There are two
possible popular locations for this event and both have credible support.

...behold, two of them were traveling that same day to a village called Emmaus... while they conversed... Jesus Himself drew near and went with them. But their eyes were restrained, so that they did not know Him. And He said to them, "What kind of conversation is this that you have with one another as you walk and are sad?" Then the one whose name was Cleopas answered and said to Him, "Are You the only stranger in Jerusalem, and have You not known the things which happened there in these days?" And He said to them, "What things?" So they said to Him, "The things concerning Jesus of Nazareth, who was a Prophet mighty in deed and word before God... today is the third day since these things happened... and certain women of our company, who arrived at the tomb early, astonished us. When they did not find His body, they came saying that they had also seen a vision of angels who said He was alive... Then He [Jesus] said to them, "O foolish ones, and slow of heart to believe in all that the prophets have spoken!... He expounded to them in all the Scriptures the things concerning Himself. Then they drew near to the village [Emmaus]... they constrained Him, saying, "Abide with us, for it is toward evening... And He went in to stay with them. Now it came to pass, as He sat at the table with them, that He took bread, blessed and broke it, and gave it to them. Then their eyes were opened and they knew Him; and He vanished from their sight.

LUKE 24:13–31

THE CHURCH OF EMMAUS. EL QUBEIBEH. PALESTINE

This is the main altar in the Church and shows Jesus, Cleopas and Simeon breaking bread together. This is thought to be the most likely place for Jesus' meeting with His followers.

Therefore, having been justified by faith, we have peace with God through our Lord Jesus Christ, through whom also we have access by faith into this grace in which we stand, and rejoice in hope of the glory of God. And not only that, but we also glory in tribulations, knowing that tribulation produces perseverance; and perseverance, character; and character, hope. Now hope does not disappoint, because the love of God has been poured out in our hearts by the Holy Spirit who was given to us.

ROMANS 5:1–5

SUNRISE OVER THE SEA OF GALILEE. ISRAEL

After Jesus' resurrection, He was seen by hundreds of people. With so many witnesses, it is hard to deny the reality of His victory over death.

...if you confess with your mouth the Lord Jesus and believe in your heart that God has raised Him from the dead, you will be saved. ROMANS 10:9

Don't trust the clouds. . . trust the sunshine! ROBERT H. SCHULLER **193**

THE PRIMACY OF SAINT PETER, SEA OF GALILEE, ISRAEL

This simple chapel by the Sea of Galilee commemorates the place where, it is believed, Jesus revealed Himself again to his disciples after His resurrection.

...when the morning had now come, Jesus stood on the shore; yet the disciples did not know that it was Jesus. Then Jesus said to them, "Children, have you any food?" They answered Him, "No." And He said to them, "Cast the net on the right side of the boat, and you will find some." So they cast, and now they were not able to draw it in because of the multitude of fish. Therefore that disciple whom Jesus loved [John] said to Peter, "It is the Lord!" Now when Simon Peter heard that it was the Lord, he put on his outer garment... and plunged into the sea.

JOHN 21:4–7

Bad news can be turned into good news when you change your attitude. ROBERT H. SCHULLER **195**

Jesus said to them, "Bring some of the fish which you have just caught." Simon Peter went up and dragged the net to land, full of large fish... although there were so many, the net was not broken. Jesus said to them, "Come and eat breakfast." Yet none of the disciples dared ask Him, "Who are You?"—knowing that it was the Lord. Jesus then came and took the bread and gave it to them, and likewise the fish. This is now the third time Jesus showed Himself to His disciples after He was raised from the dead.

JOHN 21:10–14

INTERIOR, THE PRIMACY OF SAINT PETER, SEA OF GALILEE, ISRAEL
The rock shelf in the foreground is called the Mensa Christi ("Christ's Table") and is believed to be the rock on which Jesus had breakfast with His disciples.

Attempt great things for God—expect great things from God. ROBERT H. SCHULLER

THE CHAPEL OF THE ASCENSION, MOUNT OF
OLIVES, JERUSALEM
This chapel on the top of the Mount of Olives is thought to mark
the location where Jesus ascended into heaven.

*[Jesus said] ...it was necessary for the Christ to suffer and to rise
from the dead the third day, and that repentance and remission
of sins should be preached in His name to all nations, beginning
at Jerusalem. And you are witnesses of these things..." And He
led them out as far as Bethany, and He lifted up His hands and
blessed them. Now it came to pass, while He blessed them, that
He was parted from them and carried up into heaven. And they
worshiped Him, and returned to Jerusalem with great joy...*

LUKE 24:46–52

THE GOLDEN GATE (EASTERN GATES), JERUSALEM

The arches shown on this wall rise above the Eastern Gates, though the gates themselves are now covered by a graveyard. Many think the gates will not be opened until it is time for Jesus to return. If you look into the clouds here, there seems to be an outline of a person kneeling down to pray. When we humble our hearts and call out to God, He will show up.

[Jesus said] "For as the lightning comes from the east and flashes to the west, so also will the coming of the Son of Man [Jesus]be... the Son of Man will appear in heaven, and then all the tribes of the earth will... see the Son of Man coming on the clouds of heaven with power and great glory. And He will send His angels with a great sound of a trumpet, and they will gather together His elect from the four winds, from one end of heaven to the other."

MATTHEW 24:27–31

[Jesus said] "Let not your heart be troubled; you believe in God, believe also in Me. In My Father's house are many mansions; if it were not so, I would have told you. I go to prepare a place for you. And if I go and prepare a place for you, I will come again and receive you to Myself; that where I am, there you may be also. And where I go you know, and the way you know"... "I am the way, the truth, and the life. No one comes to the Father except through Me."

JOHN 14:1–6

Change your thoughts and you can change your world.   ROBERT H. SCHULLER   **199**

The Holy Land Today

Mediterranean
Sea

LEBANON

SYRIA

ISRAEL

PALESTINIAN TERRITORIES (West Bank)

JORDAN

EGYPT
(Sinai)

Negev

Dead
Sea

Sea
of
Galilee

Golan Heights

Jordan R.

PALESTINIAN
TERRITORIES (Gaza)

Miles 0   10   20
Kms 0   10   20   30

Biskinta
Beirut
Alayh   Zahlah   Riyaq
Barr Iiyas   Sirghaya
Al Qutayfah
Saydnaya
Dumayr
Duma
Sidon
Dahr Al Ahmar   Damascus
Habbush
Najha
Tyre
Sa`Sa`
Qiryat Shemona
Ghabaqhib
Nahariyya
Al Qunaytirah
Acre
Ash Shaykh Miskin   Shahba
Haifa
Qiryat Motzkin
Tiberias
As Suwayda
Nazareth
Afula
Dar'A
Irbid
Busra Ash Sham
Pardes Hanna
Hadera
Janin
Tisiyah
Netanya
Al Mafraq
Nablus
Kefar Sava
Rosh Ha'Ayin
Tel Aviv-Jaffa
As Salt
Az Zarqa
Karama
Amman
Ramallah
Jericho
Ashdod
El Muwaqqar
Jerusalem
Madaba   Jiza
Ashqelon
Libb
Gaza   Ibbim
Hebron
Dhiban
Yatta
Khan Yunis
Qasr
Rafah
El Mazra'A   Rabba
El Qatrana
Beersheba   Arad
Karak
Dimona
Safi   El Huseiniya